PEOPLE
CAN'T DRIVE YOU
CRAZY
IF YOU DON'T
GIVE THEM THE
KEYS

Other books by Mike Bechtle

Confident Conversation
Evangelism for the Rest of Us

PEOPLE
CAN'T DRIVE YOU
CRAZY
IF YOU DON'T
GIVE THEM THE
KEYS

DR. MIKE BECHTLE

Revell

a division of Baker Publishing Group
Grand Rapids, Michigan

Published by Revell
a division of Baker Publishing Group
P.O. Box 6287, Grand Rapids, MI 49516-6287
www.revellbooks.com

Printed in the United States of America

Library of Congress Cataloging-in-Publication Data
Bechtle, Mike, 1952–
    People can't drive you crazy if you don't give them the keys / Mike Bechtle.
        p.   cm.
    Includes bibliographical references.
    ISBN 978-0-8007-2111-4 (pbk.)
    1. Interpersonal relations—Religious aspects—Christianity. I. Title.
BV4597.52.B43 2012
158.2—dc23   2012020284

Unless otherwise indicated, Scripture quotations are from the Holy Bible, New International Version®. NIV®. Copyright © 1973, 1978, 1984, 2011 by Biblica, Inc.™ Used by permission of Zondervan. All rights reserved worldwide. www.zondervan.com

Scripture quotations labeled NASB are from the New American Standard Bible®, copyright © 1960, 1962, 1963, 1968, 1971, 1972, 1973, 1975, 1977, 1995 by The Lockman Foundation. Used by permission.

To protect the privacy of those who have shared their stories with the author, some details and names have been changed.

The internet addresses, email addresses, and phone numbers in this book are accurate at the time of publication. They are provided as a resource. Baker Publishing Group does not endorse them or vouch for their content or permanence.

Published in association with the literary agency of Alive Communications, Inc., 7680 Goddard Street, Suite 200, Colorado Springs, Colorado 80920.

13   14   15   16   17   18   19   14   13   12   11   10

To Tim
What could be more rewarding than to have a son
you respect and love?
Your influence in my life has been priceless.

Contents

Acknowledgments

Someone said that if you took all the crazy people in your life and laid them end to end . . . it would be best to just leave them there. In a book about "crazy people," the list of contributors could be longer than the book itself. Listing them by name would be impossible (and dangerous).

But I have to acknowledge them. Thanks to all the crazy people in my life. You know who you are. Well, actually, you probably don't. But without you, the book would have no reason to exist. Strange as it sounds, I'm grateful.

At the other end of the continuum are those life-giving souls who keep me sane. Without them, this book wouldn't exist either. They're the ones who shape my life and give me hope in the midst of the craziness. The list would be much longer than the crazy people, and any expression of thanks seems inadequate.

Specifically, I'm indebted to a choice few who have walked with me through this journey of a third book:

Dr. Kristine McCarty has been my writing buddy throughout the process. She worked on her doctoral dissertation while I worked on this book, and our weekly contact for encouragement and accountability have been priceless for staying on schedule. Without her eyes on my progress, I would have been scrambling to meet deadlines. I've learned the privilege of teamwork and partnership. Thanks, friend.

They say lightning never strikes twice in the same place. For me, it struck three times. Working with Dr. Vicki Crumpton of Revell on all three of my books has been like winning the lottery repeatedly. It was my dream to work with her again, and I'm grateful that my agent, Joel Kneedler of Alive Communications, made that happen. Both of them are masters at finding an author's voice and putting their own passion into a project. I'm humbled to have both of you in my court.

Dr. Dennis Chernekoff graciously put his professional counseling expertise on the manuscript, making sure that no one would read my ideas and immediately jump off a tall building. There's a lot of security in being reassured by an expert and a friend. Thanks for taking the time, Dr. C.

My family provided a constant reminder of what matters most and kept the whole project in perspective. Sara, Tim, and Brian just bring joy into my life by existing, and my grandkids remind me that crazy people aren't the norm. What a gift you all are . . . !

In the end, Diane has been my biggest cheerleader, encourager, and friend. Because of her love and input, I didn't have to do this project alone. We're closer at the end of this book than we were at the beginning, and her partnership has been my most treasured part of this journey. You have my heart, which means it's in the best possible hands. I love you.

Thanks, God, for walking with me—always.

Part 1

Stuck in a Crazy World

1

I'm OK, You're Crazy

Your day starts innocently enough. The kids will be in school, your spouse will be at work, and since you worked extra this weekend, you actually have the day free. It feels like a gift because it happens so rarely. You can run errands, catch up on a few phone calls, and tackle that project you haven't had time for. You might even get a chance to read or to relax on the patio.

High expectations. High anticipation. Low stress. It's going to be a good day.

Then it happens . . .

- Your child wanders down the stairs, crying because she just threw up in the hallway (and she has pink eye).
- Your spouse rushes back into the house and says, "My car won't start. I need you to take me to work . . . and pick me up this afternoon."
- Your mother appears at the door unannounced.
- Your mother-in-law appears at the door unannounced.

- Your child flushes the toilet and everything backs up into the tub.
- Your friend from church calls—the one who always has a crisis and never takes a breath while telling you about the latest one.
- A message from your boss says, "I know I told you to take the day off . . . but our client is only going to be here today. Could you drop by about one o'clock for just an hour?"

People are driving me crazy!

We all have crazy people in our lives. If we're not in the middle of some dramatic situation, we probably just came out of one—or are about to go into one. It seems like there's always something going on that causes stress. In those rare stress-free moments, we start worrying about what's going to happen next.

Where there are crazy people, there is drama. No matter how hard we try to eliminate that drama, it keeps coming back—as long as those people are in our lives. Some people bring the drama innocently, while others seem to have a personal mission of demolishing our sanity.

We all have an emotional set point where we're most comfortable. It's that position where things are going well, we feel good, and no one is messing up our lives. When they do, we subconsciously take control of whatever we can to get things back to normal. We try to fix the problem, change the person, or alter the situation.

If it works, we go back to our set point and are comfortable again. If it doesn't work, we feel agitated, worried, and stressed. We're out of our comfort zone, and all we can think about is getting back where we belong.

That's *drama*. It's anything that makes us feel unsettled. And it always has something to do with people—people who drive us crazy. Crazy people and drama go hand in hand.

We assume that life would be better without all the drama. But when you talk to people about the life you've lived, what stories do you tell? It's all about the drama, not the routine. We describe a person's life as "colorful" when they've lived through harrowing escapades.

We talk about the thrilling adventures we had on vacation, not the daily routine of reading through the morning paper. Reality shows are edited to feature the moments of drama, not the hours of boredom.

A retired police officer I know described his career as "years of fairly routine activity punctuated by a few moments of sheer terror." Somehow, drama adds richness to our lives when we look back on it. It's the pain in the *present* we try to avoid—the pain that often comes from relationships.

Drama can take different forms and have different results in our lives. Having your schnauzer throw up on the carpet just as guests arrive causes drama, but not as much as having your kitchen on fire. Your spouse meant well when he accidently put your favorite wool sweater in the dryer, but the fact that it now fits your canary causes another kind of stress—balancing your feelings about his good intentions with the unfortunate results of his choices.

In both cases, drama results from what others say or do.

What Craziness Looks Like

Crazy people bring drama into our lives, but not all dramatic events affect everyone in the same way. For our purposes, we're looking at drama that involves some of these characteristics:

First, it involves our *emotions*. It doesn't matter what the event was or what a person said or did. The thing that makes it dramatic is how we *feel* about it. That's why two people can be stuck in the same traffic jam and be late for the same appointment, but one person is upset while the other one isn't. The event isn't really the problem; it's our response to the event.

Second, it usually involves *people*. When others don't meet our expectations, we experience drama. They cut us off in traffic, show up late, or respond to us with sarcasm. If a specific situation bothers us, it probably has something to do with people. On a blistering hot day, we blame the utility executives for charging such high rates for electricity to run the air conditioning, and then we blame our boss for not giving us the raise so we can adjust our thermostats.

Third, it's often *unexpected*. We're caught off guard because we didn't see the event coming. We don't plan for serious illness, the loss of a job, or the midnight phone call from the police about our teenager.

Fourth, it's *personal*. A lot of crazy things happen in the world, but not all of them impact us. We're talking here about the ones that directly take us out of our comfort zone. It's one thing to hear about a company president arrested for embezzling retirement funds; it's another when you work for that company and those are your retirement funds.

Fifth, it's often *exaggerated*. This isn't always true, but we often blow up a situation in our minds beyond the reality of the event. When your daughter isn't home ten minutes after her curfew, you're a little irritated. A half hour later, you're angry. An hour later, you panic. An hour after that, you're terrified and calling the police. When she finally walks in the door, you're wavering between relief and homicide.

It's a Control Issue

Our discomfort with a situation varies depending on how much control we have. If we can do something about it, we tend to be OK. The car gets a flat tire; we get it fixed. The toilet overflows; we call a plumber and clean up the mess. We speak harshly to our kids when we're tired; we apologize.

It's those situations that we can't fix or those people we can't change that make us the most uncomfortable. When the doctor uses the word "incurable" and "cancer" in the same sentence, drama takes on a whole different meaning. When a good friend turns on us and betrays our confidence, we have no guarantee that our response will "make it all better." When a boss is simply unreasonable and won't listen to logic, we might not be able to change him.

What about those situations? How can we get rid of that drama?

It's like a dance between two people. We try to stay in step, but we aren't sure exactly what the other person is going to do. When they make a move we're not expecting, we scramble to respond in a way that keeps both people on their feet. They respond to our response, and the dance continues back and forth as each person tries to negotiate the differences.

The Most Common Concern

A woman observed a man in a grocery store with a screaming, wiggling toddler in the seat of the shopping cart. The boy was totally out of control, trying to grab things off the shelf and yelling constantly. As the man moved up and down the aisles, he calmly repeated, "Billy, it's OK. You can do this. You can handle this. You don't have to get upset. Stay calm, Billy—it's OK."

The woman was so impressed by his demeanor that she felt she had to compliment him on his control. "I'm sorry to intrude—but I just wanted to tell you how impressed I am at the way you've been talking to little Billy."

The man responded, "Oh, my son's name is Jeremy. I'm Billy."

I teach seminars for a living. Several times a week I'm in a corporate or hotel conference room helping people discover ways to manage their time and life. We talk about discovering what really matters most and basing our daily choices on those values. Participants think through practical ways to arrange their personal and professional lives to accomplish the things that move them toward that goal.

At the end of the day, I'm approached by participants with questions about applying the concepts to their unique situations. The question I hear most frequently is reflected in Madelyn's concern:

> I really love this, and I'm excited about putting it into practice. But I work for a boss who just doesn't get it. I can try this, but she just wouldn't go for it. She's demanding and unreasonable, and she just

doesn't get it. This all sounds good, but I'm stuck in a no-win situation. I don't feel like I have any options.

Sound familiar? You could replace "boss" with "spouse," "friend," "in-laws," "parent," or just about any other crazy person in your life who brings you drama. The bottom line is that no matter what you do, there is someone else keeping it from working.

My response to that common concern provides the structure for this book. I generally suggest a three-step process:

1. First, try to change the situation. Explore every possible avenue to impact the other person's behavior or alter the conditions. It might involve a careful conversation with that person in a nonthreatening environment, or coming up with a creative solution to a problem. It might involve negotiating with that person about a mutually beneficial way of dealing with the issue.

2. If you've tried everything possible and the situation isn't going to change, you're left with the second step—changing your attitude. The question becomes, "What can I do to change the way I respond or handle the situation so it's not constantly eating me alive?"

3. In some instances, it might be appropriate to leave the situation. If you get to a place where your boss isn't going to change and you simply can't handle it anymore, you might consider looking for a new job or transferring to a different part of the company. Too often, though, people choose that option before working to change the situation and their attitude. Their immediate, reactive response is, "I quit." But that should usually be the final resort when other possibilities have been exhausted.

That third option isn't always appropriate. I'm not suggesting that people simply end a long-standing relationship with a family member because they're tired of the drama. Many people jump too quickly to this option before working hard on the relationship.

Here's an example:

Let's say that my house is the traditional family gathering place for Thanksgiving dinner each year. It's the biggest house and is centrally located. I love these people, but I'm a basket case by the time it's over.

Uncle Joe doesn't like turkey, so I always have to include ham as well. No one offers to bring anything, which means I pay for it all. Tina says she can't come but shows up anyway with two rather unusual friends. It takes days to clean the house and get everything ready, and everyone disappears to the football game when it's time to clean up. Instead of gratefulness, the only comments are about the dressing having too many raisins.

Here's how I might approach the three options:

1. Can I change the situation? If I'm committed to having Thanksgiving at my house, I can try to come up with alternatives:
   * Have Uncle Joe bring his own ham.
   * Send out an online invitation with sign-ups for food.
   * Hire a cleaning person to help get the house ready.
   * Disconnect the cable from the television.
   * Serve raisins in a separate bowl.
2. If people won't go along with my suggestions, I can work on having a good attitude where I accept the realities of people's behavior.
3. If I get to a point where the stress of the situation is affecting my health and my sanity, I can change the environment:
   * Simply say, "I'm not having Thanksgiving at my house this year. Just let me know where you'd like to meet, and I'll be there to help."
   * Reserve a room at a local restaurant and let the family know how much it will cost per person.
   * Arrange to be on a Thanksgiving cruise with friends or immediate family.
   * Arrange to have the house tented for termites.

It's a practical application of the Serenity Prayer: "Lord, grant me the serenity to accept the things I cannot change, the courage to change the things I can, and the wisdom to know the difference."

Where We're Headed

In the first section of this book, we'll explore the possibilities for influencing a situation with the crazy people in our lives. There are no guarantees, but many of the approaches people use are ineffective. We need a new set of keys to unlock those relationships.

"But what if the keys don't work and the locks are broken beyond repair? And what if we're in a situation where we can't simply walk away?"

In the second section we'll look at the characteristics and attitudes we can build into our lives that tend to influence others the most. It's not about things we do as much as who we become. We'll focus on the seven most effective "keys" to handling crazy people—personal qualities and responses that keep us from becoming victims of other people's weaknesses.

The final section deals with the practical realities of relationships: when it's appropriate to leave, and suggestions for connecting with others in a healthy way.

So, Is "Drama-Free" Possible?

Martin Luther supposedly said, "You might not be able to stop the birds from landing on your head, but you can keep them from building a nest in your hair." We can't stop various events from happening, and we can't choose what other people do or say. Crazy people will always be present in our lives.

"Drama-free" doesn't mean getting rid of the drama or the people who create it. *It means being free from its debilitating effects in our lives.* This book is about getting free—not letting our lives and attitudes be controlled by the choices of others.

Fruit and Faith

Becoming free from the craziness of others isn't an act or a role-play. We don't have to pretend to be something we're not or to feel things we don't feel. It's about actually becoming different on the inside.

If we want peaches on a peach tree, we don't glue peaches onto the tree. We make the tree healthy and it produces peaches naturally. In the same way, we don't have to try to act nicer or more patient in our drama-filled relationships. We need to become nicer or more patient on the inside. It takes too much energy to fake it.

When we've been driven by drama and affected by others for years, it might seem hopeless. But this isn't just a set of self-help techniques. It's all about genuine change, where we actually become the type of people who have the inner strength to handle the craziness that others bring into our lives.

We can't overlook the impact of faith on our lives, either. I've found that my resources for solving relationship problems are limited, but trusting God to build character in my life is the greatest source of strength. My relationship with him prepares me to have better relationships with others.

A Bold Promise

Here's my promise to you. If you read through this book, are open to challenging your perspective, and commit to the journey of personal growth, you'll learn to be free from the tyranny of other people's choices and behaviors. It doesn't mean there won't be pain in those relationships, but you'll have the resources to deal with those situations without simply ignoring them or glossing over the injury. You'll build stronger relationships, find more joy in every area of your life, and not be a victim of the weaknesses of others. You'll be responsive instead of reactive. It will impact both your physical and mental health.

You'll be *free*.

2

The Problem with Believing We're Right

"I can't believe we trusted him!"

He had our money, as well as the project we had given him to do. And he had simply disappeared. No one else knew where he was either—even the people who had worked in nearby booths at the swap meet for years.

Since he always rented the same space for his work, he had been easy to find. He had done top quality work for us in the past, and we had been thrilled with the results. We could pick up an inexpensive scenic print at one of the art dealers at the event and take it to him. A week later the print was mounted and coated with a unique, heat-applied finish that made it look like a piece of art costing a small fortune. It was waterproof, damage-proof, and protected from just about anything that could happen.

Except theft.

Other than that, he seemed like a genuinely nice guy.

We had gone to the huge swap meet about thirty miles from our house one Saturday morning, specifically looking for a picture to hang in the guest bedroom we were decorating. We sipped the coffee we had stopped to purchase as we wandered through the outdoor gallery. Our choice was obvious and perfect, and we immediately took it to the seller for his finishing touches. We agreed on the price, paid for the work, and arranged to meet him the following weekend.

Emotion: Deep satisfaction. We made a good choice. The coffee tasted great as we enjoyed the morning's casual activities.

The following Saturday, we stopped for coffee and strolled through the parking lot. But when we got to his space, it was vacant. We walked up and down several neighboring aisles to make sure we had the right one, but he was gone.

We assumed he was sick and couldn't make the event. We understood, but it would have been nice for him to have called and saved us the trip.

Emotion: Somewhat annoyed, but understanding. At least we had good coffee.

We managed to mentally put it aside during the next week and planned for another trip to pick it up the following Saturday. Again, we stopped for coffee, almost to convince ourselves that we were OK and that we would have a nice morning. As we walked through the parking lot, we said, "Wouldn't it be a bummer if he was gone again this week?"

That turned out to be prophetic. The space was once again empty, and no one had seen him. We tried to stay calm, reassuring ourselves that something must have happened since he had been so trustworthy in the past. But at the price of gas, these trips were becoming more than just inconvenient. They were cutting into the money we had saved by shopping at this swap meet.

Emotion: Bummed. Bordering on angry, but trying to give him the benefit of the doubt. Too much drama—we don't like drama. The coffee seemed to get cold quickly, and we tossed the half-empty cups.

Another week passed. We didn't talk about it, but the unfolding drama was always in the background. We planned to go back on

Saturday, when we would determine if our fears had any foundation. "Sure, he'll be there this time . . . and he'll let us know what went wrong."

We had his phone number on the back of the receipt. Just to make sure, I called and left a cordial message: "Hi, we were in a few weeks ago and left a picture for you to mount for us. You mentioned that it would be done the next Saturday, but we couldn't find you that day— or the next Saturday as well. So we're planning to drop by tomorrow and just wanted to make sure everything's OK and that we can get our picture. It is kind of a long drive, so we're just checking before we come. See you tomorrow morning."

The phone didn't ring. We drove the thirty miles to the swap meet. We didn't get coffee. Coffee is something you get when you're happy and having a relaxing morning. We figured we'd get coffee after we picked up our picture and everything was good.

He wasn't there.

Emotion: Anger at him for not getting in touch with us. Anger because we had been duped. Anger because he had our picture and our money, and obviously had skipped town with our stuff and probably stuff from a bunch of other people as well. Anger at ourselves because we had trusted him. Anger at the fact that we had driven 240 miles over four Saturdays. Anger at the drama. Too much drama, involving raw emotions and trust issues. Anger at the fact that we were going to have to figure out what to do about it. Plus, we hadn't had any coffee, which made us even grumpier.

By the time we got home, I had calmed down enough to make the phone call. I decided to be polite but firm in my voicemail message: "I'm calling again about the picture. You haven't returned our calls, and it's hard to keep from thinking the worst. We need to hear from you and find out when and where we can pick up the picture. Goodbye."

We were gone the rest of the day, but his return message on our machine told us that he had called within an hour of receiving our message. "Uh, this is the guy from the swap meet." His voice was shaky. "I'm really sorry about everything, and I'll arrange for you to pick up your picture." The shakiness turned to sobs. "We found our infant son dead in his crib a couple of weeks ago. They said it was sudden infant death syndrome, I think. He was our only son . . . I just don't know what to do . . . I'm really sorry . . . somebody is taking all my pictures to his warehouse, and you can pick it up there." His voice trailed off before he disconnected: ". . . I'm sorry. . . ."

Emotion: Deep, deep hurt for his tragic loss. Shame for the assumptions we had made. An insatiable desire to reach out to him.

I called back and left a message of connection and compassion. The picture wasn't important anymore. We saw him differently—a man who had been devastated and needed arms of healing around him.

We were drained from the emotional roller coaster. It had been a month filled with drama. But as unpleasant as the drama was, it couldn't compare to the drama he had experienced.

The Problem with Perspective

As much as we say we dislike dramatic relationships, we're drawn to them on reality television. When the "villain" emerges, the show gets interesting and we can't tear ourselves away. The drama builds ratings, and we talk about the episodes with friends the next day. We love to watch crazy people—as long as we don't have to interact with them personally.

We all have drama in our lives, but many people are controlled by that drama. Their lives and emotions seem to be at the mercy of everything that happens around them. Without realizing it, they have become victims of the weaknesses of others and their lives are controlled by those people.

Thinking back over the swap meet events, I've often thought about the drama surrounding it. Where did my emotions come from in that process? Since I didn't have all the facts, did the real drama come from the situation or from my interpretation of the situation? Could I have handled it differently? What about the next time something like that happens? Is there a way to respond differently?

I realized that my problem was threefold:

1. I didn't have all the facts, so I made assumptions.
2. I decided those assumptions were accurate.
3. My emotions were based on assumptions that were untrue (but I didn't know they were untrue).

Notice that the whole process took place inside my head. In this case, I was upset that another person was messing up my life. But if I had known the truth, I could have made better assumptions and experienced different emotions. In fact, that's exactly what happened when I finally discovered the truth.

That's the problem with our perspective; we always assume we're right based on the information we have.

In most of this book we'll be talking about how to respond when people make crazy choices that mess up our lives. But the place to begin is with *our* perspective. No matter what the other person does, it's our perspective that determines how we feel and respond.

Our perspective is the lens through which we interpret everything we see in the world around us. It's like wearing glasses. Unless they're really dirty, we don't notice the lenses; we see *through* those lenses. If the lenses have the wrong prescription, things look distorted. When that happens, we don't question the lens; we just assume that the object we're seeing is really distorted.

People don't start out crazy at birth. In their first few years, they decide if the world is a safe place or not. That's where their lenses are shaped that they use the rest of their lives to learn to function in society. If they have positive and secure experiences early on, they can feel safe and build positive relationships. If they have negative experiences, they see the world as unsafe and develop skills to negotiate the land mines of life. When that happens, their ways of coping might appear crazy to others.

For example, rich people often assume that poor people would be happier if they became wealthy, and that wealthy people would become unhappy if they became poor. Yet some of the wealthiest people in society are the most unfulfilled because they haven't found true happiness. Some of the poorest people experience true joy in close relationships and simple lifestyles.

A story made the rounds on the internet several years ago that described this scenario:

An American businessman was on the pier of a small coastal Mexican village when a small boat with just one fisherman in it docked. Inside the small boat were several large yellowfin tuna. The American complimented the Mexican on the quality of the fish and asked how long it took him to catch them. The Mexican replied, "Only a little while." The American then asked why he didn't stay out longer and catch more fish. The Mexican replied that he had enough to meet his family's needs. The American then asked, "But what do you do with the rest of your day?" The Mexican fisherman said, "I sleep late, I fish a little, I play with my children, I take a siesta with my wife, I stroll into the village each evening where I sip some wine and play guitar with my amigos—so I have a full and busy life, Señor."

The American laughed and scoffed at him. He said, "You know, I have an MBA from Stanford, and I can help you. You should spend more time fishing, and with the proceeds you could buy a bigger boat, and with the proceeds from the bigger boat you could buy several boats, and eventually you'd have a fleet of fishing boats, and then instead of selling your catch to that middleman over there, you could sell directly to the processor, eventually opening your own cannery. You could control the product; you could control the market. You could control all the processing and distribution. And then, of course, you'd need to leave this little fishing village and move to Mexico City. Then you'd move to LA and eventually New York City, where you would run an expanding enterprise."

The Mexican fisherman said, "But, Señor, how long will this take?"

The American replied, "Maybe fifteen to twenty years."

"But what then, Señor? What after the fifteen to twenty years?"

The American laughed and said, "Ah, that's the best part. Because after that, when the time is right, you'd sell your company stock to the public, you'd become filthy rich, and you'd make millions."

"Millions, Señor —then what would I do?"

"Ah," the American said, "then you could retire, move to a small coastal fishing village where you could just sleep late, fish a little, play with your kids, take a siesta with your wife, stroll into the village in the evening where you could sip wine and play guitar with your amigos." (Author unknown)

The Bible says that any argument makes sense until we hear the other side (Prov. 18:17). That doesn't mean we're wrong and the other person is right. But it means that our perspective may be incomplete. The only hope we have for dealing with crazy people is to base our assumptions, actions, and responses on *truth*.

It takes humility to question our perspectives. Until we look through the other person's eyes, we don't have the complete picture.

The Chances for Change

Some people have been impacted by the craziness of others for so long, they can't imagine living any differently—or even believing it's possible. Can it be different? Is it possible to live in freedom from the tyranny of other people's actions?

The answer is "Yes." The chances of changing someone else's behavior might be as realistic as getting your teenagers to clean their rooms: possible, but not likely (and not without a fight). But we can always choose how *we* respond to others. It might be unfamiliar territory, and it's a different way of thinking that needs to be learned and practiced. But it's possible.

This is a book about hope. We won't be able to eliminate the drama in our lives or escape all the crazies. But we can actually learn to live responsively instead of reactively, being positive when others are negative.

- We'll learn the keys to living in community with the crazy people we can't escape, being victors instead of victims.
- We'll learn how to discover and accept our unique temperaments, operating from a position of strength exactly the way we were created.
- We'll explore the impact that others have on our lives and learn what to do with the reactions we have around them.
- We'll talk about what we can do to impact those relationships and how to handle it when they won't change.
- We'll learn how to harness the power of emotions in relationships instead of being threatened by them.
- We'll study the life characteristics that equip us to handle the drama in an honest, realistic way.

Living in hope comes from seeing things the way they really are. It starts with checking our own perspectives before trying to influence the perspectives of others.

It's about changing from the inside out.

3

How Relationships Work

Imagine what it would be like if everyone had a TV monitor attached to their head where we could see exactly what people were really thinking. Their words would say one thing, but the screen would reveal their true thoughts:

What they say: "What a great color on you!"
What they think: "I remember when that color was in style."

What they say: "I'm glad we got to spend some time together."
What they think: "Now I won't feel guilty until we have to do it again."

What they say: "Your new baby is adorable."
What they think: "Wow—rough time in delivery, right?"

It seems like it would be helpful if we knew exactly what other people were thinking. Instead of having to guess their responses, we would have an honest look at their true feelings. Knowing the truth would make communication a lot easier, right?

To some degree that would probably be true. We would love to read other people's minds. But how would you feel about having a screen on *your* head, where you weren't able to hide your real thoughts? Well, that's a different story.

If we have someone in our lives with whom we can be totally transparent, we realize what a gift that is. We care enough about them to tell the truth, but we do it in love. They care enough about us to do the same. Those relationships are priceless and rare.

Several years ago, my wife and I were considering moving to another city. It wouldn't have been a big move, since the city was about thirty miles away. We could still do our work from there and would still be close to our kids and their families, but we would live in an area we had always been drawn to. Housing prices were similar, so it would have been a move we could easily make.

But we decided to stay where we were, an area where we've lived for over twenty years. The new city was far enough away that we would have to start a whole new set of relationships. We'd done that before, but we realized the value of our current friendships. They aren't casual friends; they are deep relationships that have been built by two decades of life experiences. We've supported each other through raising our children, juggling job priorities, and facing personal challenges together.

Yes, we could make new friends. But we knew how much time and energy it took to develop the depth of connection that was so important to us. Like diamonds, those relationships develop with time and pressure. They have great value to us, and we weren't willing to give that up.

The Birth of a Relationship

Relationships are like rivers. The deepest rivers with the most force and beauty can take your breath away. But follow those rivers to their sources. They start high in the mountains with individual drops of water that form into shallow rivulets, becoming gentle streams that build in volume as they become raging currents at the bottom.

Relationships begin with brief encounters. Two people who don't know each other meet for the first time. Their first words are usually a greeting, a social convenience to overcome inertia and get a conversation started. We really don't know anything about the other person, so we begin taking in verbal and visual data to form an impression of them. Subconsciously we think something like, "Based on how they look, how they're dressed, their eye contact, hairstyle, mannerisms, and tone of voice, I'm guessing this is what they're like." Of course, we're probably way off base, but we have to start somewhere.

From that point on, we listen and look for clues to tell us if our evaluation is right or wrong. The longer we interact, the more data we have to clarify our impressions of them.

So we start shallow: "How are you?"

"Fine, how are you?"

It might sound trite, but it's a legitimate way of testing the waters. It doesn't work to go too deep at the beginning of a relationship: "Hi, I'm Bonnie. How much do you weigh?"

The Growth of a Relationship

As we continue to interact, those droplets begin to merge as we learn about the other person and look for common ground. Gradually we begin to discover each other's interests and priorities. The more we talk, the better we are able to decide if we can connect well with that person.

The more we connect, the more we let that person into our lives. Strong relationships don't start strong; they grow life-on-life through a series of experiences where trust is built.

Once we trust that person and have a relationship, we get comfortable. The river grows deeper and moves faster. We develop our "set point" where the relationship works well. We have unspoken expectations of what the relationship will be like.

But the closer we become, the more the relationship will be challenged. Like a river overflowing its banks and moving in new directions, people are unpredictable. When someone we know goes against our expectations, we're uncomfortable and we want to move things back to our set point.

The further they take us from our set point and the more they violate our expectations, the more uncomfortable we are. We know we're not the problem, so we may decide that the other person is certifiably crazy.

Five Myths about Relationships

"But it's so obvious," we say. "Why don't they just get it?"

When it comes to relationships, it's easy to wonder why things don't go the way we plan. "After all," we say, "we're being completely logical about issues. If those other people would just take the time to listen to our perspective, they would immediately understand our point of view and everything would be fine. Why don't they just get it?"

They're probably thinking the same thing about us.

Relationships don't fit into neat little structures; they're messy. We can plan how to approach different people, assuming that they'll respond in a certain way. But since they are unique individuals, they have their own unique way of responding. We never know how they're going to respond until they do. Any time we base our actions and choices on what we think the other person will do, we'll be frustrated.

We often base our relationships on inaccurate principles or myths. These aren't intentional choices we make; they're just assumptions we've adopted that get in the way of healthy relationships.

1. If I can convince someone of the facts, they'll respond differently.
Trying to change someone's emotional response with logic is like fighting a kitchen grease fire with water. They just don't mix and can cause even more flare-ups.

2. *I'll never be happy until this relationship is fixed.*

This perspective allows the other person to be in charge of our emotions. It's a reactive response that robs us of the freedom to grow and thrive. We become victims of another person's weaknesses and choices.

3. *If they would just get right with God, everything would be OK.*

While a strained relationship with God can cause havoc in a person's life, there's no guarantee that a healthy spiritual life will solve every relational problem. People are in process. We're all growing, and we will never reach perfection in this life. Have you ever watched church people disagree?

4. *It takes two people to improve a relationship.*

If one person won't cooperate in working on a relationship, it's going to be tough to make it a strong, vibrant connection. But that doesn't mean we have to be trapped by dysfunction. When we learn healthy ways of responding, we're taking control of our emotional thermostat. We haven't fixed the other person, but we've lessened their impact on our lives.

5. *If I'm patient and hang in there, they'll eventually come around.*

False hope damages both parties in a relationship. We want the other person to change, and we hope and pray for the best. But the other person is responsible for their own choices and the consequences of those choices. If we think that our being consistent will make them change, we're taking responsibility for them. If they don't change, we've set ourselves up for disappointment.

Five Truths about Relationships

So, what *do* we know about relationships?

1. *The people we spend the most time with create the most drama.*

Different people impact us in different ways. A casual acquaintance might irritate you, but you don't see them that often. On the other hand, the person who sits next to you at work every day, lives in your house, or comes to every holiday celebration can turn your emotions upside down.

2. *Relationships take work.*

Someone said, "The best things in life are free." That might be true in terms of money, but it takes a focused, concentrated commitment to overcome the craziness that other people bring into our lives.

3. *Relationships take time.*

On television, many relationships seem to be healed with one or two conversations. In real life, those conversations happen—but they're only a small part of a much longer process. Just as a physical wound takes time to heal, emotional issues don't find resolution overnight.

4. *The past doesn't have to predict the future.*

In a long-term relationship, change might feel hopeless. Your crazy sibling has acted a certain way for years, so you assume that you "can't teach an old dog new tricks." But the only chance for hope in a relationship is to leave room for the possibilities. There won't be guarantees, but there is always hope.

5. *You don't have to be a victim.*

In a toxic relationship, it's easy to feel sucked dry by another person. It's true that they might never change, and there could always be drama in the relationship. But we don't have to let them mess up our lives.

Options for Dealing with Crazy People

The more crazy people we have in our lives, the greater the potential for drama. The more drama there is, the more uncomfortable we are. In an effort to get back to our set point, we usually assume one of the three options we talked about in chapter 1:

1. Convince the crazy person to change.
2. Live with the craziness.
3. Get the crazy person out of our life.

The first option is worth considering but is often unrealistic. If we put all our hopes on another person changing to fit our expectations of the relationship, we'll be sorely disappointed. We can't force other people to change. If we count on it, we're setting ourselves up for consistent emotional pain. We can influence change, but we can't demand it. A mom may force her son to sit in a chair for a while as punishment; however, the child may think, "I'm sitting down on the outside, but I'm standing up on the inside."

The second option is a skewed version of a healthy response that often leads to a martyr complex: "I guess this is just my lot to bear in life. I'll never be happy, because this person is stuck in my life and will never change." The last part of that statement is often true: they're a permanent fixture and they'll always be crazy. But living as a victim is optional. We can choose how we respond.

The third option works in some situations, but it's tough in others. You can't always choose your co-workers or your boss. Family members will always be family members, even if they live across the country. When your two-year-old is driving you crazy, you can't say, "Look, you're not living up to your part of the bargain here. You're making me crazy. It's time for you to go. We're having a garage sale this weekend . . ."

When we can't change a situation and we can't leave the situation, we can choose our response to the situation. It's a responsive approach that keeps us from becoming victims of another person's choices.

Hope for Healing

Someone said that if you ever find a perfect organization, don't join it—if you do, it won't be perfect anymore. The same holds true for any relationship. Author Kathy Collard Miller shares about meeting the man who would become her husband, thinking he was her knight in shining armor and their marriage would be perfect. Then she started seeing the rust spots.[1]

Wouldn't it be nice if we could wave a magic wand and have all that drama disappear? It won't happen. That's the problem: we're all imperfect people. As long as we live in an imperfect world surrounded by imperfect people, we're going to deal with drama in relationships.

Some people pray for God to straighten out all their relationships. But usually God doesn't just zap people so they think and act differently. Instead, he gives us wisdom in dealing with those relationships.

Having healthy relationships doesn't mean other people are going to be perfect or life will be drama-free. It doesn't mean that everyone else is going to change for the better. It means that we work on our side of the relationship, no matter what happens on the other side. We don't change them; we change ourselves.

When we become healthy, we can have *hope*.

Part 2

Changing Someone Else

4

Stop Yelling at the
Toaster Oven

Because I live in a large metropolitan area, I spend a lot of time driving. I'm usually working in a different company every day, often fifty to a hundred miles from my home. That means there will be traffic both directions. You can't drive in Southern California without experiencing traffic.

When we first moved here from Phoenix, someone advised, "Don't let the traffic get to you." I thought I understood about traffic until the first day I had to drive into downtown Los Angeles. When the freeway was at a standstill, I assumed there must be a terrible accident somewhere ahead. But then I realized there was no accident; it was just a normal rush hour.

So I had two options. One would be what a lot of drivers do, which is to get angry and frustrated. They pound the steering wheel, drive recklessly, and yell at other drivers around them. Their emotions are being managed by something they can't control: the traffic.

I realized that the first option (getting upset at the traffic) was futile. That left me with the second option: changing my own response to the traffic.

In the morning, I've learned to leave extra early before the worst congestion hits, then relax at a coffee shop near my destination. In the afternoon, I can't avoid the traffic. But I plan alternate routes and listen to traffic reports, and I also have relaxing music or audio books to listen to while driving. I can't change the traffic, but I can protect my emotions from being hijacked by that traffic.

It's important to know what we can control and what we can't. When we confuse the two, we set ourselves up for frustration.

For instance, I can choose the color of the car I purchase, but I can't control if someone else likes it or not. I can control the choices I make in raising my kids, but I can't control the choices they make as they move toward adulthood.

When we see people we care about making bad choices, we want to fix them so they'll make good choices. But what happens when they don't?

It's unhealthy to be at the mercy of what someone does or doesn't do. We can't control the choices and attitudes of others. The only thing we really have control over is our own choices and attitudes. When we take responsibility for our own choices, we gain greater influence in other people's lives. When we focus on things we can't do anything about, we lose influence with others. We give away our joy and our sense of self to their weaknesses.

One city I visit fairly often is about sixty miles from my home. I usually drive there early in the morning to beat traffic, then hang out at the local coffeehouse until it's time to go to my seminar location.

At this particular coffee spot, there is a small group of men who meet daily on the patio. Ranging in age from their midsixties and up, they drink their coffee and share opinions about what's going on in the world and what needs to happen to solve each situation. They talk about war, politics, the economy, and things happening around the world. I've seen them there over a number of years, and people sit on the patio just to be entertained by their strong opinions.

I don't know what these men do the rest of the day, but it seems like they've gotten really good at putting significant emotional energy into things they can't do anything about—which means they're not putting that energy into things they can actually change. I've often wondered what they might accomplish if they quit talking and focused on making a difference. It wouldn't have to be something world-changing, just taking action on something where they can have influence. When people do that, their influence begins to grow over time.

Can People Really Change?

Is change actually possible? The simple answer is yes—people *can* change. No matter how long they've been a certain way, there is always hope. People can grow and change as the currents of life take them in new directions. We don't want to throw up our arms and say, "It's hopeless. They'll never change." We might be the catalyst in that person's life, influencing them to become more than they currently are.

The bigger question is, "*Will* they change?" There's no simple answer for that one, because we don't know what choices they might make in the future. There is *always* hope, but there are *never* guarantees. If we're going to avoid becoming victims of other people's craziness, it's critical to operate from a dual perspective: *hope* and *realism*. Without hope, maintaining the relationship seems futile. Without realism, we set ourselves up for the probability of disappointment. Without balancing the two views, we lose our ability to make choices that are healthy.

Yes, people can change. People *might* change. But it's their choice; only they can do the changing. We can't take responsibility for their choices. When we do, we feel the frustration that comes when other people don't cooperate with our plans, and we end up yelling at the toaster oven.

The option isn't just to escape the relationship, though that might be appropriate in some situations. Too often people run away to escape the pressure but never address the issues that caused the pain in the first place. Years later, they still carry those unresolved issues with them and are still being eaten alive by bitterness.

Reasoning with the Unreasonable

When our minds tell us one thing but our emotions tell us something else, which do we believe? Unless we challenge our emotions, they always trump logic.

I experienced this recently on a short business trip. The flight was only an hour, and we were about five minutes from landing when we hit the rough air. The turbulence wasn't too bad, and it had been a fairly smooth flight until then. The man across the aisle was trying to read but was obviously uncomfortable. With each bump, one hand would grip the armrest while the other crumpled the magazine he was holding. I could see him suck in his breath and hold it, then try to distract himself by reading.

Earlier that day, I heard a news item about air safety. It described the statistical chances of dying in a commercial plane crash versus dying in a car accident. Over fifty years, your chances of dying in a car accident are about one in one hundred. Your chances of dying in a plane crash are about one in 10.5 million.

I could have leaned across the aisle and tried to convince my fellow passenger that he was statistically safe and had a much greater chance of an accident while driving home from the airport after we landed. I could have shown him graphs and data to demonstrate the truth of my words. But he would still have been gripping the armrests whenever the plane shifted.

When people experience strong emotion, they can't hear logic. Have you ever tried reasoning with a frustrated spouse or an angry teenager? How did it go?

In *Switch: How to Change Things When Change Is Hard*, Chip and Dan Heath use the analogy of riding an elephant.[1] The rider represents logic, making analytical decisions about where he wants to go. His conclusions make sense and he has the data to back them up. But the elephant represents emotions. The rider might be able to yank on the reins and move the elephant by logic for a while, but he soon becomes tired from the effort. Then the elephant simply goes wherever it wants.

Most of the time, the elephant trumps the rider—emotions trump logic. For us, the only time the rider wins is when we have a crystal clear picture of who we want to be and make conscious, deliberate choices in that direction.

Who's in Control?

Look over the following list of things we typically find stressful. For each one, decide if you can control it or not:

1. Where we work
2. Other people's opinions
3. The things we eat
4. Late flights
5. What we do with our free time
6. The stock market
7. Who we spend time with
8. Wars around the world
9. Our choices
10. The weather
11. Our attitudes
12. What time the sun comes up
13. Where we go on vacation
14. Other people's dysfunction
15. How we respond to other people's dysfunction
16. Job security
17. What we have for breakfast
18. How long the toaster oven takes to toast bread

We could argue that some of these—for instance, "who we spend time with" or "job security"—could fit in both categories. It's true that our work situation might seem to dictate those issues, or we could gain new skills that would enable us to make changes in those areas. But for the most part, the odd-numbered items are things we can control, while the even-numbered ones are out of our control.

Have you ever yelled at the toaster oven because it was taking so long, or at the computer because it took five seconds for a website to load instead of two?

Life is filled with examples of things we can and can't control. Most people have trouble separating the two, and it causes stress. Our expectations are unrealistic when we try to change the unchangeable.

The Solution

What can we control? *Ourselves.* What can we not control? *Everything else.*

Our frustration comes from trying to control people and circumstances that are out of our realm of control. The key to surviving crazy people is to determine what we have control over and put our energy there. We can't change others, but we influence them when we change ourselves.

I learned this lesson as a teenager in Phoenix. Like any sixteen-year-old, I was proud of having my license and considered myself to be a pretty good driver. Normally, I tend to be fairly laid-back. But when I started driving, I found a side of my personality I had never seen before.

It started the first time someone cut me off in traffic. With a line of cars in front of me and no one behind me, a car rolled into the lane ahead of me and drove about ten miles per hour, causing me to jam on my brakes to avoid hitting him. "He's crazy," I thought, and I was angry with him. So like any mature driver, I immediately started tailgating him. I figured he would notice what I was doing and feel remorse for cutting me off.

It didn't happen.

I encountered a lot of crazy drivers over the next few weeks, and I became more and more upset when it happened. I actually got to a place where I was angry before I started the car. I was thinking, "I wonder who it will be today?"

One day, after a similar incident, I was fuming at another driver and tailgated him as punishment. I pulled up next to him at a signal and glared at him. But he didn't notice that I was glaring, which made me even angrier. My horn didn't work, so I couldn't get his attention. I got even angrier, since I was trying to punish him and he didn't know it was happening.

Then I realized what was happening. He was fine. I was fuming. The only person I was punishing was . . . myself. I had allowed my emotions to be controlled by the exact person I *didn't* want controlling them. I had become his victim and he didn't even know it.

Have you ever been angry with someone and couldn't let it go? Maybe you were hurt in a relationship years ago and haven't seen the person since. But you're still living as a victim of that person's behavior.

Holding anger toward someone in that way is like taking poison and expecting the other person to die.

We need to become different people in our responses to others, building character traits that allow us to handle their craziness without becoming victims. When we become different, people will respond to us differently. But most important, we'll have the strength of character and the boundaries that allow us to be emotionally healthy, no matter what others do.

"I Hear You're Expecting . . ."

A lot of the discomfort in relationships comes from our own expectations. When we decide what a person is like during our first contact with them, we assume it's accurate. We form those first impressions quickly, and we believe them to be true.

The problem is that we're evaluating the person from a one-sided perspective. We don't know their perspective, so we assume it's the same as ours. It's like we're looking at things through our own lenses—our background, culture, education, experience, language. But the other person is doing the same thing, assuming that we're thinking the same way they are. So we both end up with unrealistic expectations of what the relationship will be like.

Have you ever believed something about someone and then gained new information that changed your belief?

If I have to jam on my brakes when someone cuts in front of me without signaling on the freeway, my first thought is that they are incompetent, rude, and aggressive. I might feel strong emotion and make all kinds of assumptions about their character and competence.

But I've done the same thing to other people accidently when they're in my blind spot. I might think I was looking carefully, but I don't realize I've cut them off until I hear their horn as I merge dangerously in front of them. I didn't do it maliciously, and I'm not being aggressive. But seeing their response in my rearview mirror tells me they don't know what really happened. They're making the same assumptions about me that I often do about others.

We interpret the actions of others as malicious when they might be totally innocent. And how we interpret their actions is what upsets us.

Communication: The Key to Accurate Understanding

I say, "It's going to be hot today." I grew up in Phoenix, so "hot" means a dry 117 degrees. But if you're from Atlanta or Anchorage, "hot" takes on an entirely different meaning.

I'm looking through my lenses in a conversation. I know what I'm thinking (117 degrees), and I listen to you through those lenses, assuming that we're on the same page. I'm listening to you, but it's from my point of view.

Here's the problem: *We're both doing the same thing.*

If both of us are assuming that we understand what the other person means with their words, we're both going to be wrong. We see our side clearly and wonder, "It's so obvious—why don't they get it?"

The solution is to look through each other's lenses. I need to realize that your perspective is different than mine and try to understand how you see things. That doesn't mean I have to agree with you; it just means I want to see what you see. If we each take the time to understand where the other is coming from, we lay a foundation for an effective relationship.

It's even worse when there's a third person involved. If I talk to someone about you behind your back, I'm adding their perspective to my own, reinforcing my assumptions about your motives. Without talking to you and trying to understand your view, we move ever further away from realistic connection.

Proverbs for Perspective

"But that sounds impossible," you say. "If I've spent my whole life looking through my own lenses, and the other person does the same thing, how can we learn to do it differently?"

Good question. Fortunately, there's a good answer. The Bible isn't just a book about religion; it's a book about relationships, and it's filled with practical suggestions for making our own relationships work. Here are some examples:

- Don't bring up issues that have already been dealt with in the past. (Prov. 17:9)
- Don't stretch the truth, but be honest in your conversation. (Eph. 4:25)
- If someone gets upset, don't respond with anger. (Prov. 15:1; 25:15; 29:11)
- Listen carefully, and don't interrupt until you've really heard the other person. (Prov. 18:13)

- Look for ways to encourage the other person. (1 Thess. 5:11)
- Pick your battles; avoid arguing whenever possible. (Prov. 17:14)
- Put energy into seeing things from the other person's point of view. (Phil. 2:4)
- Spend a lot more time listening than talking. (James 1:19; Prov. 10:19)
- Think before you respond to someone. (Prov. 15:28)
- Watch carefully what you say so you don't get yourself in trouble. (Prov. 21:23)

If we want to learn how to get the best use out of our new car, we read the manual provided by the manufacturer. If we want to have effective relationships, we glean insights from reading the instruction manual from the One who designed relationships. These principles are powerful in all of our relationships, including the crazy ones.

That doesn't mean that if we do the right things and follow these principles then other people will automatically get their act together. We can't control how they respond, but we can control how we respond to them. Principles like these can be the foundation on which we base every relationship, no matter what the other person does.

Notice that all of the above principles give instruction to us, not to the other person. It's all about what *we* do in relationships, no matter what others do. That means we develop ways of relating that we use every time, knowing that we might or might not get the response we're looking for.

Lifeguards are a good illustration of this. They're trained in the most effective techniques for saving lives, and they use those techniques consistently. They know that they won't save 100 percent of the people they go after, but it doesn't stop them from trying.

So in a sense, it's all about us. We are responsible for *our* choices, actions, and attitudes, and we can actually change those. That's not true about other people. We can't force them to do or feel anything.

What *can* we do, then, in the lives of others? We can use the most effective tool we have for getting other people to change: *influence*.

5

The Impact of Influence

Recently I heard someone say, "You become like the five people you spend the most time with." That idea has captured my thinking the past few days, and two questions have surfaced:

1. With whom do I spend the most time?
2. Have I really become like them?

I spend the most time with my wife. We have our own unique personalities, but thirty-four years of marriage has us finishing each other's sentences and responding to things the same way. Our interests have merged over the years, while we still have our unique areas of focus. In a healthy relationship that's a good thing.

I also spend a lot of time around people I work with, friends at church, and members of a small group that meets regularly. As I've thought about it, I do see how we've rubbed off on each other. We carry hints of the "scent" of each other's lives.

Those changes haven't been intentionally crafted but seem to just happen as we spend time together.

So if the statement is true, it leads to two more questions:

1. Are those five people becoming more like me?
2. Is that a good thing?

The Power of Influence

I've realized that I choose not to spend much time with people who are trying to change me. If they take me on as a project to "fix," I don't respond well. But when they simply enter my life and accept me unconditionally, I become a different person because of their influence. Without my realizing it, their acceptance influences me to become like them.

That's why it's important to be intentional about who we hang out with. It's comfortable to connect with people who are just like us, but we don't change or grow. To really stretch and develop as a person, we need to intentionally choose close relationships with people who are further ahead in certain areas of life.

In other words, find people of all ages whom you admire and want to be like, and hang out with them.

What happens in those relationships? They're not giving you formal instruction or walking you through a curriculum; they're just being themselves while you watch them in different life situations. Without even realizing it, you're learning how to handle those situations in your own life. They model effectiveness for you.

They're not forcing you to change; they're influencing you. You become different by being around them.

Think back over the years to the people who inspired you to be better—to do something you didn't think you could do, or to aim higher than you would have on your own. It might have been a teacher, a coach, a grandparent, or a family friend. Somehow, they made you believe in yourself. They came alongside when you were struggling and said, "I believe in you."

How did that feel?

Maybe you had a painful childhood and weren't given the nurturing you deserved. Today you still feel the bondage of those early defective relationships. When someone finally believed in you, that person probably stands out in your memory like a shaft of sunlight breaking through storm clouds. They may not even know it, but their presence in your life made a difference. They didn't put together a formal course of instruction. They just came close enough to influence you.

That carries over into all of our relationships. People are watching us, whether we know it or not. The closer we are, the more they will pick up what they see. How we handle life situations influences how they handle life situations.

You Can't Force Change

My wife Diane loves hydrangeas. They're a striking flower that grows in spheres of color, usually shades of pink or white. They can also be a beautiful shade of blue—but not naturally.

Diane wanted blue flowers. She had two alternatives for trying to make that happen:

1. *She could use force.* She could grab the flower around the stem and say, "Look, if you don't bloom with blue flowers, you're going to find yourself on the rough side of the compost bin."
2. *She could use influence.* If she applies a carefully measured amount of aluminum sulfate to the soil, the blooms will usually be blue.

It's true with any type of gardening. We can't force things to grow, but we can influence their growth with water, nutrients, cultivation, and other forms of care. If we provide the right environment, there's a lot better chance of healthy growth.

Relationships are the same way. We can't force people to change. The more we try, the more frustrated we'll become.

President Dwight Eisenhower was once asked what he believed about motivating people. He picked up a string that was sitting on his desk and tried to push it ahead of his fingers, but it obviously didn't work. His fingers moved first, and the string followed. He pointed out that if you try to push people ahead, it leads to frustration.[1] The only way to motivate others is to go in front and provide an example, and they will often follow.

It's not our job to fix other people. But we often find ourselves trying to do exactly that, and it's frustrating when they don't cooperate.

So, what *is* our job?

Many books on relationships talk about protecting ourselves from the weaknesses of others, setting boundaries, and keeping our distance. There is definitely a place for that perspective, because we can't be victims of another person's dysfunction. But that doesn't mean we shouldn't try to make a difference. The Bible talks a lot about influencing others, which means they stay on our radar. We can't force them to change, but we can seek to influence them. The issue isn't how *they* respond; the issue is how *we* treat *them*.

It's a threefold perspective:

1. We try to influence the other person instead of trying to force them to change.
2. We are realistic in our expectations, knowing that we can't direct their behavior.
3. We choose a healthy way of relating to that person, developing the appropriate boundaries to keep from becoming a victim of their choices.

Expectations vs. Expectancy

Sharon has always had a painful relationship with her father. Though he never verbalized his displeasure, her brothers always seemed to get his attention and focus while she had to make an effort to be recognized. She felt like an "unavoidable delay" in his schedule. Now, as an adult, Sharon struggles with how to relate appropriately to her father. They've never been close, but she feels obligated to fix the relationship and "make it all better." Unfortunately, the more she tries, the more disappointed she becomes in his responses.

Should she just give up? Should she keep trying, hoping that something will happen? Should she do it out of guilt, knowing that she's supposed to "honor her father"?

Our expectations get us in trouble. When a relationship is unhealthy, we often try to rescue it. The closer the relationship, the more we hope it will improve. But if I make it my mission to change you, I'm setting myself up for disappointment. It messes with my emotional set point if you don't do what I'm expecting, and the emotions follow. Expectations always lead to pain when they're not met.

A healthier perspective is to come with *expectancy* rather than expectations. With expectancy, I don't know what's going to happen. I can be honest about my concerns and acknowledge my desire to have the person change, but I'm not demanding that things have to turn out a certain way. I don't know how things will turn out.

Instead, I'm watching to see what happens, being sensitive to changes that I might overlook. That person may never change, and the relationship may never be healed. But if I can view things realistically, I'm building a foundation for how to make choices in that relationship—no matter what happens.

We Have a Choice

Our brain tends to run on autopilot. Things happen between us and others, and we rarely stop and think through the healthiest way to respond. Our default reaction is to "fix" what seems to be broken instead of to "influence."

When you think of the people who have had the greatest impact in your life, what percentage of them had an agenda for you and what percentage had influence? While both may be factors, it's probably weighted on the side of influence.

We need to become intentional about influencing others. It allows us to take responsibility for our side of a relationship, while giving others the freedom to make their own choices. It's hard to influence a relationship and push our own agendas at the same time. When we consciously influence, we put ourselves in a position where we have to give up forcing the other person to change.

When I think about the people who have influenced me, I realize that none of them had an agenda to change me. They simply cared enough to get close, and I was able to observe their lives firsthand. As a result, I became a different person.

John Adair was my youth pastor when I was in high school. His hobby was rebuilding old pianos. I was fascinated with music and expressed an interest in what he was doing. So he invited me to spend time with him in his garage, working alongside him to learn the skills of construction, finishing, tuning, and maintenance. I learned about pianos from his knowledge, but I learned about life from our relationship. At a time when I was facing the uncertainty that teenagers feel about life, John believed in me. I can't pinpoint a lot of specific things he said, but I remember how I felt when I received his affirmation. When I couldn't believe in myself, I borrowed belief from him. He didn't force me; he influenced me—and much of who I am today came from that relationship.

Influence means living a healthy emotional life in close proximity to others. It means that we intentionally put ourselves in relationships where we can be life on life with them. My friend Jim refers to it as "rubbing fur" with others. We don't have to have an agenda; we just have to care enough to connect.

We shouldn't place expectations on those relationships, because then we would become discouraged when people don't respond properly. But we can have expectancy, knowing that our influence in their lives will have some type of impact. We might not see how that impact displays itself, but we can be certain it will occur.

Balancing Hope and Realism

We want people to change, especially the crazy ones. Everything inside us wants them to be different. They've thrown us off our emotional set point, and we wonder if our emotions will ever get back in balance.

It's a fine line between two ends of a continuum:

1. Hope (that they'll change)
2. Realism (knowing they might not)

Both ends can exist together, which is why it's possible to keep from being thrown too far from our emotional set point. When we've tried so many times to impact people's lives with no results, it's easy to give up. Realism acknowledges that it might not get better.

But no matter how bad it gets, there's always hope.

Brad and Linda have a twenty-five-year-old son who is the source of their pain. Their son has chosen a path that goes against the values and priorities they tried to instill in him, which strains their relationship. Conversation is shallow when they get together, and he seems to be making no progress in finding direction and purpose in his life. They pray for him, stay in contact with him, but have pretty much given up hope. To keep their sanity, they have accepted the fact that things probably won't change.

If they believe their son will always follow the same path, it's a realistic perspective to protect their emotions. But it's also realistic to know that God loves their son as much as they do (more, actually). They might be out of fuel, but God isn't.

That doesn't mean the son is going to change. It simply means that God hasn't given up and will be intimately involved with him throughout his whole life. Brad and Linda might not have reason to expect change in their son's future, but they can trust God to always be working in his life.

That's the difference between expectation and expectancy. With expectation, we're waiting for something specific that we want to happen, and we'll be disappointed if it doesn't. With expectancy, we release our own agenda in a person's life, allowing changes to happen that we can't control.

We can't be the quarterback of another person's life. But we can be members of his team, supporting and influencing him to become a better life player.

6

Can I Fire My Family?

Your next-door neighbors painted their house fuchsia. Your boss is sabotaging your career, and a co-worker comments on your private phone conversations from the next cubicle. Your best friend drains your energy with stories about his cat, and the people at church complain about your singing. Even politicians and celebrities whom you've never met curdle your milk whenever you watch the news.

But no one can grab your emotions and wring them out more than family.

The closer people are to you, the more havoc they wreak on your emotions. A co-worker might have more impact than a stranger, and close friends affect us even more. But family members can have us planning a move to a skunk farm to improve our conditions.

We can change jobs and move away from friends, but family members are in our lives to stay (and often without our consent). We didn't ask them to be part of our family, but there they are with all their craziness.

It often happens when two people fall in love. Over time their personality differences begin to emerge. No one sees it coming, so it adds drama to the relationship. But they're committed to each other, so they work through those issues. The relationship gets stronger and they decide to marry.

That's when the craziness starts, because they meet each other's families for the first time. Suddenly, they realize that they are going to be related to a group of people they've never met and will have to spend holidays with them. They're not just marrying their intended; they're joining their family too.

Those early family gatherings reinforce their fears. As they spend time with these people, they feel like they're eavesdropping on a side-show act from the circus. But if the relationship is going to work, they have to learn to get along with the clowns as well as the wild animals.

The closer they get to the wedding, the more drama surfaces. Both of their families have different ideas of what's important for the ceremony and reception, and the couple deals with the stress of family negotiation. If it really gets uncomfortable, they think, "We just have to make it through the wedding and we'll be OK. After all, we don't have to live with them."

That's true in most cases. But the engagement and wedding are only a dress rehearsal for the rest of their lives. Each holiday that comes around brings expectations from all sides that have to be negotiated. It's like when a bunch of kids are running around the house chasing each other and you think, "Somebody's going to be crying in about five minutes."

But the biggest stress on a couple's relationship comes when the first grandchild is born. Suddenly, people on both sides of the family want access to the child and have their own expectations of how their grandchild should be raised. They might genuinely want to help, but they often intrude in the couple's life without being asked.

When my wife Diane and I started mentoring young married couples at our church, we would get calls from them saying, "Can you come over for coffee sometime soon? We have something we want to talk to you about." We could almost always guess what the topic would be based on what stage they were at in their relationship:

- If they were newlyweds, it had something to do with their own relationship (squeezing the toothpaste in the middle of the tube, leaving clothes on the floor, flossing in public, etc.)
- If they had been married for several months, it had something to do with in-laws (why they keep interfering, why they keep making unsolicited suggestions about how to be a better wife or husband, etc.)
- If they just had their first baby, it had something to do with the expectations of the new grandparents (being omnipresent, suggesting the only "right" way to handle the new baby, being upset because the couple is choosing different ways of doing things than the way they did it, etc.)

It's almost like the parents on both sides say, "Well, we raised you this certain way and look how you turned out. Of course you'll want to do it the way we did." If the couple goes against the patterns from either side, it's taken as a slap in the face.

You Can't Choose Family

We can't choose the family we're born into. We spend our whole lives learning how to negotiate those relationships, but it's not by choice. We relate because we're related.

We can choose who we marry, but we don't get to choose their family. We can try to ignore them or say, "They're not really my family. They're his/hers." It's a nice idea, but it doesn't work. When you marry them, their family becomes your "in-laws." Literally, it means they are "in law" (legally) your family too.

When your siblings, parents, or children marry someone, you become related to strangers because of that choice. You don't ask for it; it just happens.

That's what makes family drama more intense than other relationships. With other people, we know we could just end a relationship, change jobs, or move away, and the relationship is no longer there. But with families, it's easy to feel trapped. If a crazy person is suddenly in our life by default, it changes the dynamic between us and them.

There are five characteristics that define family relationships: proximity, history, patterns, feelings, and expectations.

Proximity

The closer we live to someone, the more demands there seem to be on our relationship with them. If our in-laws live on the other side of the country, we don't have to deal with as much face-to-face drama as we would if they lived two blocks from our home. But when they visit, they stay for longer periods of time, possibly under our own roof. They might also have higher expectations for staying in touch than we'd like.

I've often thought of making a plaque to put on our guest room wall with the verse from Proverbs that says, "Seldom set foot in your neighbor's house—too much of you, and they will hate you" (Prov. 25:17). Diane doesn't think it would match the décor.

When family members live nearby, they stay in their own house. But we'll probably encounter them more often.

The greatest potential for drama happens under our own roof. Our commitment to our immediate family helps us get through the crazy moments, but we're with each other 24/7. Invite an elderly parent or cousin to move in, and it gets even crazier (for both the family and the "guest"). The proximity can add drama but without the commitment that exists between immediate family members.

History

Even if our family is messed up, we grow up thinking it's normal. It's all we've ever known. Because it's our only model of how people interact, we don't know a different approach. Since it's always been that way, we assume it's OK and nothing will change. That assumption directly impacts how we communicate with family members.

A lot of husbands and wives have told us about the drama with their spouse's family. They spend time with them and notice the communication patterns that seem unhealthy. So they take it upon themselves to try and change those patterns, attempting to "fix" something that has existed for decades.

When they're with crazy Aunt Alice, for example, they start replaying the old tapes in their head about what she's always been like, and that becomes the foundation for how they interact with her. They might try to stay friendly with her or ignore her or become defensive. They might keep all conversations at a surface level to avoid conflict. In other words, they choose from their own menu of unhealthy responses.

History brings us to where we are right now, but it doesn't have to dictate how we respond in the future.

Patterns

When our kids are little, we watch how they develop. We see their interests, temperaments, and patterns of behavior. After fifteen years or so, we think we've got them figured out and we know how they'll turn out as adults.

But then they move in a whole new direction. It's not necessarily bad, just different. Diane says it's like we write a storybook about our kids' lives over the years, and in their mid-teens we write the rest of the book—including the ending. Then over the next few years, they tear out our ending and write their own.

Kids are human. So are other family members (yes, even crazy Aunt Alice). That means we can try to predict their future behavior based on how they've always been, but we'll probably be wrong. Relationships are dynamic because people are always changing. We can't plan our responses until we see what they say or do.

Feelings

When relationships are unhealthy, they hurt. The reason they hurt is because we care. If we didn't care, they wouldn't hurt.

That's why people you care about the most can hurt you the most. A lot of people try to shut down their feelings in a painful relationship in order to protect themselves. That can be appropriate in some situations, but it eliminates the possibility of healing. Our feelings provide the fuel for working on a relationship. If we stop caring, we've given up on the relationship.

Expectations

Proximity, history, patterns, and feelings all lead to expectations. Based on past experience, we decide what will probably happen in each relationship. Then we believe those assumptions, and we're taken off guard when the other person violates our expectations. It happens most with family members because expectations rise the closer you are to someone.

Survival Strategies for Families

Dealing with crazy family members can feel like swimming at night in a shark-infested ocean. You know the sharks are out there, and usually nothing happens. But you know there's a chance of being eaten alive. Survival in a family setting requires honesty about what's really happening, understanding several key concepts:

1. *It's not my job to fix another person.*

I'm responsible for my choices; you're responsible for yours. If I take the responsibility to make you act in a certain way, then you're no longer responsible and you're dependent on me to fix you.

I can't control what the sharks do. I'm only responsible for what I choose to do, knowing that the sharks are there.

2. People can change—but don't count on it.

When we know how another person acts, we assume they'll always be that way. But since they're human, there is always hope. Situations come into people's lives that can cause them to make new choices. We can't force them to change, but we can influence them.

There are no guarantees, however. If we count on them changing, we're setting ourselves up for disappointment and frustration. The healthy response is to:

- hope and pray that they change;
- accept the fact that they might not change; and
- avoid becoming victims while we influence their lives.

3. Escaping doesn't always solve the problem.

Sometimes it's best to leave the situation. But if we don't deal with our own issues in that relationship, we carry those unresolved issues with us. That's why people leave a painful marriage, but yet they can't let go of their bitterness even when the other person is gone. Years later the other person is still controlling their emotions, and it's eating them alive.

4. We need to talk to the person, not about them.

When we talk about someone behind their back, it's called gossip, even if it's a crazy family member. Of course, we're going to talk with each other about how to handle dynamics that are happening within the family. But there's a fine line between discussing the reality of a relationship and feeding the fire of emotion.

When someone causes pain in a family, we need to decide what to do. The key is to make sure the discussion doesn't spiral down into gossip. Healthy dialogue centers on what type of boundaries need to be set and how to respond to that person's behavior, without just rehashing their craziness over and over. We need to focus on the facts that support our feelings.

How do we stay focused on facts? By talking *to* the crazy person, not simply *about* him. Gossip never promotes healing. Truth does.

5. *We don't want to rescue or enable the other person.*

There are natural consequences in life for our choices. If we choose to stand in the rain, we get wet. If we eat too much, we gain weight. If we rob a bank, we go to jail. If we don't feel the consequences, we have no reason to change.

Sometimes, when crazy people cause pain, we try to rescue them. A teenager spends his money on concerts and electronics and doesn't have enough left to put gas in his car to get to work. We know that if he can't go to work he'll lose his job. We don't want to see him lose his job, so we lecture him about money decisions. Then we fill his tank, hoping he'll make better choices in the future. But since he didn't feel the consequences, he has no reason to change.

There's usually no need to lecture or punish. It's much more effective to just let people feel the natural consequences of their choices.

That's why we deal with crazy family members differently than other crazy people. They're in our lives whether we like it or not. We can try to influence them, knowing that they probably won't change. If they don't, we can keep from being victims of their craziness by not taking responsibility for their choices.

We still care about them. But instead of punishing or manipulating them, we simply allow them to feel the consequences of their decisions. If they emotionally or verbally abuse others, the natural consequence will be broken relationships.

The Bottom Line

Can we change crazy people? No. We can't force anyone to think or act differently. But we can influence them.

Is there hope? Yes. But there are no guarantees. I've learned that God never gives up on someone, and he's the one who is working in their lives. We need to care about the person, trust God for what he's doing, and avoid becoming a victim of the other person's choices.

How is that possible? Here's what we've learned so far:

- If we count on others changing, we'll be disappointed.
- Our attitude can't depend on what others do.
- If we escape a situation without dealing with the issues, we take the issues with us.
- Other people see things differently than we do, and we both think we're right.
- Expectations are the basis for pain. Expectancy is the basis for healing.

If we can't change another person, we must learn how to change ourselves.

Part 3

Changing Yourself

7

Why Can't Everyone Be Like Me?

Akeem was a classmate of mine in graduate school. It was his first time in America, and the first time he had ever been outside his African homeland. His language skills were perfect, his academic prowess was enviable, and his ability to connect with people and make friends was remarkable.

For the first few weeks he was excited about his new adventure, but he soon became homesick. For several weeks, his energy seemed to slide toward depression. It was subtle, but he hadn't heard from family or friends since arriving. (This was in the mid-1970s, before email and instant communication.)

But one day, he danced into the classroom with a large bag and a huge smile. He had finally received a box from home, filled with notes and treats from family and friends. The bag contained his favorite snack, which he wanted to share with his fellow students. Inside were about one hundred fried black beetles, each about two inches long. His mother had prepared this crunchy delicacy for him, and he ate them like potato chips.

We were excited for him, but he got to eat all one hundred by himself.

We thought he was crazy and couldn't imagine how someone could eat big, black bugs. But he often commented on American cultural issues that he couldn't understand. For instance, it was hard for him to comprehend Americans growing and mowing a lawn. "In our country," he said, "we don't have enough water to grow food. Here, you plant an entire yard, water it and care for it, then you harvest it . . . and throw it away. I don't understand!"

Good point. We take our culture for granted and assume that it's right. We see how other people live and think they would be much happier if they lived the way we do. But it's really not a matter of right and wrong; it's just different. It's away from our set point, so it makes us uncomfortable.

It's not just our tastes that are different; *we're* unique as well. We're most comfortable with our own set point. We assume that everybody else would be more comfortable if they were just like us and did things our way.

Extroverts assume that introverts would be happier if they were more outgoing. Introverts think that extroverts need to calm down and be more reflective. Who's right?

Donna and Phil love their friends but subconsciously think they could all use a little "touching up":

- Sarah is the quiet one. She never ruffles anyone's feathers and doesn't speak her mind very often. When she does, she usually has the deepest thoughts—but it's like pulling teeth to get her to share them. Donna and Phil describe her as "terminally nice."
- Tom worries too much. Donna and Phil love to be with him, but he usually finds the dark side of any situation. He says he's just being realistic, but they think he'd be happier if he could lighten up.
- Barry and Linda are fun to be around—in small doses. They can be the life of the party, and each could run a conversation even

if they were alone. They're lively, outgoing, and animated—the perfect party people. When walking out of Barry and Linda's house, Donna and Phil stop for a moment to enjoy the silence.

We have our set point where we're the most comfortable, so it's natural to assume that others will be comfortable there, too.
But other people are thinking the same thing about us.

Different by Design

We're all different, and it's not a mistake. God never intended for everyone to be the same, even though it might seem to be more comfortable. Just as there is variety in nature, there is variety in people.

Relational pain doesn't usually come from the areas where we are alike, but from those areas where we differ.

Imagine going to an orchestra concert and finding that the only instruments being played were violins. No brass, no percussion, no woodwinds—only violins. While a violin can produce a mesmerizing sound, we would quickly grow tired of a concert with no other instruments.

The reason we enjoy a concert is the variety of sounds that blend together. As a group, an orchestra produces a combined sound that no individual instrument can make. But in that process, you can still hear the individual instruments. It's unity in diversity; it's difference by design.

The people in our lives are like an orchestra. They're all unique, and together they provide richness to the music of our lives. Some of those people seem crazy, while others bring energy. Each makes their own "sound" and they blend together to create a symphony.

Crazy people are like a tuba gone wild. They ignore the sheet music and begin playing their own tune, overpowering the rest of the orchestra. All we can focus on is the loud, brassy tuba, and it ruins the concert for us. How can we control the tuba?

We'll talk about that in future chapters. There's one basic principle that applies, though: *the tuba will always be a tuba*. We can't change it into a flute; we have to deal with it as a tuba.

When dealing with crazy people, we can't change their temperament. Whether we like it or not, it's who they are. If we try to turn them into something they're not, we'll only be frustrated.

We can influence other people's behaviors and choices, but we can't change their temperament. "Can a leopard change its spots?" (Jer. 13:23). The obvious answer is "no." Asking an introvert to become an extrovert is like asking a golden retriever to become a spider monkey. It might seem like a good idea, but it's not going to happen.

Donna and Phil's friend Sarah will always be quiet, so they can seek creative ways to discover her deeper thoughts—perhaps through a relaxed lunch or a series of emails. Tom can learn to worry less, but he will always have the sensitive, analytical personality that looks at all the details of every situation. Barry and Linda will always be outgoing socialites, but they could be influenced to learn ways of reading the reactions of people they encounter.

When we try to influence others, we need to focus on their actions and attitudes, not their temperaments.

Heal Thyself

We can't change the way other people are wired. But it's important to accept the way we're wired as well. We can change our behavior and our attitudes, but our wiring is part of our DNA.

I remember reading a study years ago in which a hundred Hollywood celebrities were asked one question: "If you could change anything about yourself (height, looks, personality), would you do it?" The response was unanimous; all one hundred said yes.

These are the "perfect" people whom everyone wants to be like. We assume that if we could look like them and be like them, our lives would be perfect. But every one of them wanted to make a change.

Healthy relationships are based on truth. If we're going to be successful in dealing with the crazy people in our lives, we have to start by dealing with ourselves. We have to recognize the difference between things we can change about ourselves and things we can't. If we can change something, we need to act. If we can't change something, we need to accept it.

The High Cost of Forced Change

In 1999, Gallup researchers Buckingham and Coffman studied how corporate managers developed their people. The traditional view was to test employees to discover their areas of strength and weakness, then provide training in their areas of weakness to bring them up to speed. A lot of energy and dollars were spent over the years trying to make people equally competent.

They found one major problem with training people to overcome their weaknesses: *it didn't work*. They might be able to function better, but they never excelled in all areas as a result. Their research revealed that everyone has unique strengths that are hardwired *into* them, and other areas that are hardwired *out* of them. The reason people were weak in certain areas wasn't because they hadn't been trained; it was because those strengths simply weren't part of their temperament. You can train them all you want, but their weaknesses will never become strengths.

The outcome of this study was simple and logical, but dramatic. It led to a three-step approach to management:

1. Recognize and celebrate each person's uniqueness, including their natural weaknesses and strengths.
2. Let people work in their areas of strength.
3. Provide training in those areas of strength so they can specialize and excel in what they're naturally wired to do.[1]

In other words, let people be who they are instead of turning them into identical copies of each other.

Making It Personal

The place to start in managing our relationships is to recognize and accept each person's uniqueness. We'll need to decide how to handle their actions and influence their behavior, but it has to be in the context of how they're wired.

The greater challenge is to celebrate our own uniqueness. Like the Hollywood celebrities, we all have areas we'd like to change. We can do something about certain areas (our attitudes, our choices, our habits). But we can't change our temperament. It's hardwired inside of us and is part of the design for our lives. When we focus on changing the unchangeable, we're inviting frustration and disappointment to rule our lives.

Let's say we have a conversation with someone, and he starts presenting his point of view in a quick, logical sequence. It bugs us that we always think of the perfect response a half hour after the conversation has ended. We think, *I wish I could think of what to say during the conversation so I could respond logically and forcefully. I always feel like he's going to win every argument, no matter what.*

I struggled with that for years. I never seemed to know how to respond while the conversation was taking place. I would avoid confrontational situations because I knew I was going to feel backed into a corner. I always wished I could change to be more aggressive and clear-thinking in the moment.

But I realized that I'm not wired that way and never will be. As an introvert, I'm what is called an "internal processor." I take information in during a conversation, process what I've heard when I'm by myself, and respond clearly later.

Most introverts are like that. We listen carefully to what's being said, then ponder it for a while. It takes longer to formulate our responses, but those responses are usually well thought out and reflect deep thinking.

Here's how I've learned to respond: "OK, I'm listening. I'm with you. You're making some really interesting points, and I need some time to think through what you've said before I respond. Let me take a couple of days and get back with you. You deserve a thoughtful response, and I want to do that. I'll jot down some of my ideas and send you an email. Then, let's talk again."

This lets me operate from a position of strength, not weakness. I don't need to feel frustrated because I can't think quickly in a conversation. My strength is thoughtful reflection, which is probably an area of weakness for another person. When I accept that part of my temperament, I can utilize it to manage my craziest relationships without being intimidated. It doesn't mean the other person is going to change. It simply means that I don't have to feel defeated because of his uniqueness.

Fully accepting our own temperaments and the uniqueness of others can minimize the impact of drama in our lives.

Tips for Temperaments

Learning to accept everyone's uniqueness (including our own) doesn't mean they won't bring craziness into our lives, or that we have to agree with them or overlook their behavior. It simply means we start from an honest foundation. Once we're able to accept the way a person is hardwired, we're free to make healthy decisions about how to interact with them.

Here are some basic principles to keep in mind during the process:

- We need to separate their behavior from their temperament, accepting who they are while dealing with their choices.
- By accepting their temperament, it doesn't mean we're enabling them and reinforcing their craziness. We're just trying to understand them accurately.

- There's nothing wrong with a person's temperament. But there could be a lot wrong with their behaviors, attitudes, and choices. They've been making those choices for a long time, so it's not something we can easily change. We can't guarantee that they'll make good choices, but we can choose how we respond to those choices.

- It's easy to assume that if the other person changed, everything would be better. But we have our own blind spots that contribute to the chaos. We need to look inward, observing the areas of need in our own lives as well.

- The problem isn't that they're a tuba; the problem is how they're playing.

"So, why can't everyone be like me?" Because they're not us, and we're not them. We're individually crafted and unique. Hope for healing in crazy relationships begins with understanding ourselves and others, doing what we can to influence, and accepting the things that aren't changeable. As Reinhold Neibuhr prayed, "God grant me the serenity to accept the things I cannot change; courage to change the things I can; and the wisdom to know the difference."[2]

8

The Energy of Emotions

You're going to see your crazy person today. Maybe she's coming to a family gathering. Maybe you'll see her in a small group you meet with each week, or you'll be talking to her on a phone call you can't avoid. It could just be that you're going to work and she'll be in the next cubicle when you arrive.

As each minute passes, a low-grade sense of dread rises within you. Sure, the conversation could be benign. But you have history with this person, and she usually seems to know exactly how to push all the wrong buttons with you.

"Today will be different," you say. "I won't let her get to me." You set your resolve and mentally rehearse how you'll greet her. You picture yourself remaining in control of yourself, no matter what her attitude is like. *She's not going to win.*

But she wins. Thirty seconds into your conversation, she makes a casual, sarcastic comment that feels like a dagger in your spirit. Your anger rises, quickly approaching a boiling point. You refrain from saying anything, but you're hoping a piano accidently drops through the ceiling and lands on her. You feel defeated because she broke your resolve and she's in control again. Your emotions got the best of you, and your crazy person has you dangling in her grip like a bungee jump gone bad.

How Can I Stop Feeling?

Encounters like that often leave us feeling hopeless. We've tried so many times, but it feels like we'll never be able to conquer our emotions. We wonder why our crazy person is able to manipulate our feelings so easily, and we're an emotional wreck.

"I wish I could just shut off my emotions," we think. "If I wasn't so emotional, this wouldn't bother me so much."

At a basic level, that's true. But the reason we have strong emotions is because we care. If we didn't care, our emotions wouldn't be a problem.

The closer we are to someone, the more our emotions will be involved. When the president of the country makes a crazy decision, it shouldn't bug me the way it does when a family member makes one. The closer they are, the more we'll feel. It's inappropriate to have debilitating anger over events we can't control. But in a personal relationship, emotions will always be part of the connection.

Emotions are a gift from God that make our lives multicolor masterpieces. Without feelings, life becomes beige.

Doctors often prescribe antidepressants to help people cope with the "lows" in life. While these can be effective in helping a person regulate their ups and downs, one of the common side effects is that the person no longer has "highs" in their emotions, either. They feel a neutralizing effect that keeps them from feeling strongly in either direction.

Emotions are the fuel of relationships. Just as our bodies burn calories to provide energy for living, emotions provide the energy we need to work on our relationships. Emotions motivate us to take action, moving relationships from where they are to where we'd like them to be. It's kind of like pain. The stronger the pain, the more motivated we are to find out what's causing it and deal with the problem.

It's what we do with our emotions that makes the difference. Pressure comes into every relationship, pushing us away from our set point. In unhealthy relationships, people see each other as the problem and let that pressure come between them, driving them further apart.

In healthy relationships, people put the pressure on the outside, pushing them together. They see the pressure as the problem, not the other person. So they join forces to face the problem together.

There's nothing wrong with fuel. It all has to do with where that fuel is burned. When wood is burned in a fireplace, it provides warmth. When wood is burned in a forest, it produces devastation.

Reaction vs. Response

When something happens that pushes us away from our set point, we're going to feel emotion. That feeling isn't good or bad; it just "is." Reactions happen naturally and automatically and are not a problem in themselves. The problem is in how we respond.

A reaction is how we feel; a response is what we do. Reactions are automatic, but we choose our responses.

When we receive an email that touches a nerve, we'll probably feel anger. Our first thought is to reply immediately with what we're feeling. But have you ever done that and accidentally hit "send," then regretted your choice? You're trying to figure out how to break into the person's office and find his password to delete the message before he sees it.

The anger might be automatic, but what we do with that anger is the key. Instead of sending a quick reply, we might choose to process our feelings for a day or two before sending a thoughtful, appropriate response.

When someone starts yelling at us and accusing us of something, a natural reaction is to yell back and defend ourselves. That makes the other person more upset, and the conversation spirals downward.

"A gentle answer turns away wrath" (Prov. 15:1). Even though we feel like lashing out because we've been hurt, we could choose a different, more gentle response. It's hard to keep the fire going when someone removes some of the fuel.

Imagine two people standing and facing each other. Both have their hands up in front of them and are pushing against the other person's hands. Since they're both pushing, they remain standing. But if one person pulls back and removes the pressure, the other person will have to stop pushing or they'll fall on their face.

The Character of Emotions

Have you ever tried to use logic in a conversation with an angry person? We can't talk someone out of feeling, including ourselves. Holding our feelings inside is like holding a bunch of balloons underwater. Just when it looks like we have them under control, one of them pops up to the surface.

It happens when people make a major purchase, like a new car. We want to think we're making decisions based on logic: safety, gas mileage, practicality. But research has shown that we make our buying decisions based on our emotions: how we feel driving the car, how impressed others will be, how much we like the color. Once we make the decision to buy, then we need the logical features to justify that decision. We buy the car because it's red, but we convince ourselves it was a good choice because it's safe.

Feelings happen. When they do, it's dangerous to try to ignore them or pretend they don't exist. When we stuff the emotion inside, it stays there and grows and has no chance for being dealt with in a healthy way. Anger turned inward, for instance, can lead to depression, headaches, and other physical symptoms.

We all know people who yell when they get upset, and then they're fine a few minutes later. The good news is that they got the emotion out. The bad news is that everyone around them is ducking for cover or curling up in a fetal position on the floor.

There are healthier ways to handle our strong emotions. In any honest relationship, those emotions need to come out instead of staying inside. Flying off the handle with anger isn't the only way to get the emotions out. The same result comes from taking time to think before speaking and expressing clearly what we're feeling.

I violated this last weekend when I was doing jigsaw puzzles with my two granddaughters. I was working on the edges, Elena (age 4) was working on Curious George, and Averie (age 6) was assembling the man with the yellow hat. I had just collected all the straight edge pieces so I could put them together, when Averie grabbed all of my pieces that contained yellow. Several times she made choices that made it easier for her but harder for her sister and me.

Now, I adore my granddaughters. But I was starting to feel irritated at Averie's behavior. Instead of saying something, I simply got quiet and quit playing. (I've always been good at withdrawing.) When she said, "Papa, why aren't you playing?" I said, "I'm just going to watch." She said, "But I don't want to do this all by myself." I hinted at my feelings: "Well, it's just hard to do when you take my pieces, so I'll just watch you." (How's that for an adult response?)

Soon I was back in the game, helping assemble the pieces. But it bothered me for several hours because I hadn't been honest in my communication. I hadn't yelled at her, but I had stuffed down the emotion. That didn't help either of us.

Finally, we sat on the patio swing and talked about it. "Averie," I said, "I need to apologize for what happened when we were doing the puzzle. When you took the pieces I had set aside for the edges, I felt frustrated and kind of angry. But instead of telling you that, I just quit playing and you didn't know why. That was wrong, and I'm sorry. It's really, really good to tell each other what we're thinking so we know what's going on. That's what people do who love each other."

She said, "OK. Can we do another puzzle now?"

I guess being an adult doesn't guarantee we handle things properly.

Manage Your Thoughts, Manage Your Emotions

The key to controlling our emotions is to manage our thoughts. That's where our emotions come from. If I think you're upset with me, I'm going to have all the feelings associated with those thoughts. You might not be mad at all, so my emotions come from what I'm thinking, not from what is true.

A pastor told me of receiving a call from a woman who was devastated because he was so angry with her. It was a surprise to him, because he couldn't remember even having a conversation with her the previous Sunday. Evidently, he had passed by her in a crowd of people after the service and hadn't greeted her the way he normally did. In reality, he hadn't even seen her. But she felt like he had purposely ignored her and began thinking about the reasons why he might have done so. Over the next few days, her thinking escalated until she was convinced that their relationship was beyond repair.

How could she have changed her thoughts? By telling herself the truth. "The pastor didn't greet me today." (That was true.) "That's unusual, because he's always so friendly and encouraging. There must have been something going on that I don't know about. Maybe he was upset, but maybe he was just distracted. It's out of character for him, but I really don't know what's happening. Maybe I should send him a note to encourage him, and find out if everything is OK."

It's always dangerous to assume that our perceptions are accurate when we don't have all the facts. When someone yanks our chain and we feel strong emotion, we can use that as a trigger to stop and analyze our thoughts to see if they're based on truth or assumptions. Messed-up thinking mixed with strong emotion leads us to focus on the problem rather than the solution. When our thoughts are accurate, our emotions become appropriate.

Shakespeare said, "There is nothing either good or bad, but thinking makes it so."[1] Other historical writers have echoed those thoughts over the years. Even the Bible contains more than three hundred references to "thinking," for example, "As he thinks within himself, so he is." (Proverbs 23:7 NASB).

Here's the process:

1. Something happens.
2. We think about what happened and our mind decides what it means.
3. We believe our thoughts and interpretation.
4. We feel and act based on those thoughts.

The problem is in step 2. It's like a fork in the emotional road. Whatever thoughts we choose determine where we end up emotionally.

A Thoughtful Solution

So, how do we solve our thinking problems? Four steps:

1. *Pay attention to our thoughts.* When we feel strong emotion, we should stop and challenge our thoughts to see if they're based on facts or assumptions.
2. *Pay attention to our inputs.* What we watch and listen to, what we read, and who we talk to provide the raw ingredients for our thoughts. Personally, I've had to avoid talk radio while I'm driving, because the constant barrage of people's opinions impacts my attitude the rest of the day.
3. *Realize that we can change our thoughts.* Just because we feel something doesn't mean we're stuck with those feelings.
4. *Choose our thoughts instead of being a victim to them.* We can replace unhealthy thoughts with healthy thoughts. We can't just decide to "not have bad thoughts"; we have to actively replace them with good thoughts.

What type of thoughts can we replace the bad thoughts with? Things that are true, honorable, life-giving, trustworthy, encouraging, comforting, exciting, refreshing, promising, and hopeful. When those types of thoughts flood our minds and replace the negative thoughts, we have the chance to experience *peace*.

9

Seven Keys to Unlocking Healthy Relationships

Pick the craziest person in your life and place them squarely in the center of your mind. It might be painful, but they're probably already there; crazy people have this habit of camping in our subconscious mind.

That's probably the person you've thought about through the first part of this book. As you've read, you've tried to keep an open mind, applying the concepts we've covered:

- You're looking through the lens of what's true and real.
- You're choosing how you respond instead of simply reacting.
- You're deciding what you can impact in a situation and what is out of your control.
- You're analyzing the real dynamics in a relationship.
- You've learned how to influence people without the expectation of change.

- You've wrestled with the unique elements of family members who are crazy.
- You've learned how to capitalize on your uniqueness and how to recognize uniqueness in others.
- You've thought through the potential for managing your own emotions.

But you're still afraid it won't work. After all that work and energy, you really don't expect your crazy person to change.

That is a very real possibility. There are a lot of crazy people in our lives who try to pull us away from our set point. But our happiness and security shouldn't depend on whether they stay crazy or not. If we have to fix all the crazy people before we're OK, we'll be cashing our retirement checks. We'll spend our whole life driven by the brokenness of others.

Living a life free from the effects of crazy people might seem like a fantasy. But notice the key thought: *We might not be free from the presence of that person, but we can be free from their toxic impact on our lives.* Even though the other person doesn't change, we don't have to be hijacked by their craziness.

Finding Freedom

From his perspective as a concentration camp survivor, Viktor Frankl said it best: "When we can no longer change a situation, we are challenged to change ourselves."

We can't just decide that our crazy person isn't going to get to us. That's an exercise in willpower and will only last until we run out of energy. We need to work on ourselves. It's not just acting like we're OK; it means becoming the type of person who *is* OK, regardless of what other people say or do.

In other words, we shift the focus from fixing others to fixing ourselves. We put our energy into building the character traits that make us healthy people, which in turn lays the foundation for healthy relationships.

Changing ourselves has two benefits:

1. It puts us in control of our own emotional life, regardless of what others do.
2. It causes others to respond differently to us.

The first benefit is primary, which is where we're headed in the next few chapters. The second is a fringe benefit of the first. If we genuinely become different, people will respond to us differently. It might be a positive or negative response, but it will be different.

We can probably think of a time when someone changed and how we responded to them. We didn't know why, but we noticed that they didn't get upset as much as usual, or they chose kinder ways of responding, or they demonstrated more self-control. At first, we wondered what was happening and how long it would last. But when they stayed consistent over time, we began to explore the reasons behind the change. Eventually, we realized that they really had changed and that it seemed permanent. We felt differently about them because they had changed, so we interacted with them differently.

In a sense, they became a different person. When we interacted with them, we weren't interacting with the original person but the person they had become.

Years ago, one of my work colleagues had a reputation for being arrogant and self-serving, always manipulating situations to his advantage. He was friendly enough in conversations but would often talk negatively about other people behind their backs. No one trusted him, because they assumed that he would do the same with them when they weren't around.

One day, I was surprised to hear him say something positive about a co-worker. He affirmed the person's competence and skill in a situation, admitting that this person did it better than he could have done it himself. It was out of character for him and took me off guard.

When I shared his comment with the co-worker, his response was, "Are you serious? Where did that come from?"

Over the next few weeks, it happened more frequently, and the man's negative comments tapered off. Everyone was suspicious, assuming it was a gimmick to present himself more positively. But the changes became consistent. No one knew why, but he was just easier to be around.

The change had come from an "aha" moment during a training session where he came to grips with his own lack of security. He thought that the only way to build himself up was to put others down. Realizing the source of his struggle, he began a journey to genuinely change his self-perception. When he worked on changing himself, it impacted the people around him.

We can't get others to trust us until we deserve their trust. When we genuinely change on the inside, we'll relate to people differently on the outside. Others will see the change and will respond differently. That doesn't guarantee everything will be better and the relationship will be healed. But when we change, we become a different person. Others will be relating to that "new" version of us, not the old one they're used to.

Our goal is to become the people we need to be, regardless of the reactions of others. It's the foundation for avoiding the victim mentality in our relationships with crazy people.

Changing from the Inside Out

I've spent more than three decades in ministry and corporate settings. I've been able to interact with different people daily, both one-on-one and in group settings. That's given me the chance to observe how people relate to each other and the dynamics that happen in those relationships.

Sometimes I'm with people who have known each other for years. Other times my audience is a group of strangers meeting for the first time and spending the day together in a seminar.

In either case, it seems like there is at least one crazy person. In a group setting, that person might be disruptive or aggressive, monopolizing a discussion or asking inappropriate questions. In a one-on-one conversation, that person simply seems more focused on their own needs than caring about anyone around them. If we're looking for a crazy person, they're usually not hard to find.

When I talk with people who have a crazy person in their life, I usually hear one of two responses:

- The crazy person is ruining their life, and they want that person to change so they can maintain their own sanity.
- The crazy person is present in their life, but they aren't controlled by the craziness.

Over the years, I've studied these people in the second group who are not victims. I was looking for the techniques or mental gymnastics they went through to cope with the craziness. But I discovered that it wasn't a matter of techniques. Instead, they had focused their energy into the one thing they could genuinely impact: themselves.

In doing so, I recognized the seven key qualities that they had developed through the process. Though there are many areas of internal strength that build character in people, these seven consistently enable them to deal effectively with other people. We'll develop them over the next few chapters, but here's an overview:

Humility

Most people see themselves as either better than they really are or worse than they really are, with an imbalanced focus on the positive or the negative. Humility means we see ourselves accurately, accept the way we have been created, and celebrate our uniqueness.

It's easy to see others from a distorted perspective as well. When we look at crazy people, all we see is the craziness to the exclusion of every other part of their lives. We'll never be free from their grip until we see them (and us) the way we really are.

Joy

Life is filled with ups and downs. Healthy people learn how to live with both. They enjoy the good but aren't devastated by the bad. Joy means appreciating the positive experiences in life but finding meaning in the tough times as well. It means living lightly and realistically, no matter what happens.

A photographer friend tells me that cloudy days are the best for photographing flowers. The dark background provides a stark contrast to the brilliant colors. Without the contrast, the colors would simply fade together.

Perspective

Some people get their undies in a bundle about everything that happens around them. It's like they're always finding the negative, and they appoint themselves as the caretaker of everyone else's behavior. But that perspective keeps them steeped in drama.

Healthy people distinguish between what they're responsible for, what they're not responsible for, and what really matters. It's like the popular adage, "You pick your battles." As we give up trying to fix everyone, we develop a credible claim to peace.

Patience

Living in a microwave-paced society makes it hard to have healthy relationships. We're used to high drama television shows that find a satisfying ending in sixty minutes with ten commercials. Emotionally healthy people recognize that while change is possible, it doesn't happen overnight, no matter who is changing. The more we can accept that reality, the less frustration we'll feel. It's more important to embrace the present, finding our fulfillment in the reality of today instead of being driven by the uncertainty of the future in our relationships.

Kindness

Kindness is often seen as a sign of weakness rather than strength. But in relationships, it becomes the social lubricant that minimizes friction between people. If used as a tool to manipulate change in others, kindness loses its power. But when it genuinely becomes the foundation from which a person interacts with others, it provides a path to freedom. It doesn't minimize the need for appropriate confrontation, but we can do it with kindness.

Integrity

Many people make decisions based on avoiding pain and embarrassment, choosing the easy way over the right way. But without a basic moral compass, there is no foundation for a genuine relationship to grow or heal. People learn to trust us when we possess and demonstrate personal integrity, which reduces the drama that comes from a lack of trust.

Integrity is who we are when we're alone. It's when there's alignment between who we are on the inside and how we come across to others on the outside.

Commitment

An old joke portrays a couple saying, "Divorce is not an option. Maybe murder, but not divorce." In our society, we expect people to disappear when things get tough. That's why a person who sticks around when the going gets tough makes such an impact on any relationship. It doesn't mean there is never a time to leave. But for a healthy person, escaping is a last resort, not a first impulse. They know that when there is commitment in a relationship, things happen that don't occur in any other way.

These seven key traits aren't behaviors that we pull out of a toolbox when needed. They have to become part of the fabric of our life. It doesn't matter how crazy people treat us; we can respond in a healthy way. Based on these seven keys, our true character doesn't disappear under pressure.

So, Where Can I Buy These Ingredients?

If we're lacking some of these character traits, it almost seems impossible to imagine them becoming a genuine part of our lives. Fortunately, all of them are realistic. It's completely possible for them to characterize who we are.

It won't happen overnight. We can't take a pill and be all better in the morning. It's not something we work really hard at when it's not genuine. It's not what we do—*it's who we become.*

In the next few chapters, we'll look at that journey. We'll find out what it really looks like to have something new happen in our lives, anticipating the people we'll become. We'll gain hope for dealing with the crazy people in our lives without becoming victims.

God won't necessarily make your crazy people go away. But when we become different, we'll see those people differently. We'll hold the keys to unlocking healthy relationships.

10

Key #1—See Yourself Realistically

You're positive you set the alarm, but it didn't go off. Now you have a half hour less to get ready, so you fly out of bed and stub your toe. You can't be late for the meeting this morning, so you speed through your shower and start getting dressed, only to find that the clothes you had planned on wearing are still in the dirty clothes hamper. After picking another outfit, you grab a granola bar instead of breakfast and look for your keys. They're nowhere to be found. When you finally locate them, your car's battery is dead because you left the interior light on all night.

So, what do you say to yourself?

"I'm so dumb," you might say. "I can't believe I didn't check the alarm, and I forgot to do the laundry, and I didn't close the car door last night. Now I'm going to be late, and it had to happen today. I always mess up. I'm so disorganized . . ."

Sound familiar? Most of us have a tendency to evaluate ourselves through the filter of our emotions. We beat ourselves up when we have a day like that, telling ourselves that we're dumb and lazy and disorganized. If we don't challenge those emotions, we go through the rest of our day spiraling downward and those beliefs color everything we do.

The problem is that we believe a perspective that's based on emotion, not truth. If we're not seeing ourselves accurately, we have little hope for handling those emotions.

If we were telling ourselves the truth, here's what the self-talk might look like: "I have an important meeting today, and I'm going to be late. That's really unfortunate, especially since it could have been prevented if I had been a little more careful last night. I overlooked some things that led to my day starting the way it did. I'm disappointed, and I wish it hadn't happened. But I'm not stupid or lazy or totally disorganized. I'm a good person who made some mistakes last night, and I'll try to be more careful in the future."

That's what people do who see life through the lens of truth. They don't make character judgments about themselves when they mess up. Instead, they identify what they did that was a problem without seeing themselves as the problem. They'll still have strong feelings when something goes wrong, but they'll pause and sort out what is true from what is inaccurate.

That's a good description for *humility*. We often associate humility with weakness, always letting the other person have their way and avoiding conflict. But humility is a position of strength in a relationship. *It means seeing ourselves and others through the lens of truth, not through our reactive emotions.*

Making It Real

You're having a conversation with someone you want to impress. It could be a potential employer, a new friend, or a speaker you've built up the courage to approach. The conversation seems to go well, and you feel good about the encounter. But shortly afterward you catch a glimpse of yourself in a mirror and notice a chunk of spinach between your teeth. You realize it's been there the whole time and the other person never mentioned it.

It would have been embarrassing if they had pointed it out, and it would be uncomfortable for them. But wouldn't you prefer to know the truth, so you could do something about it?

Humility means not thinking better of ourselves than we really are, but also not thinking worse of ourselves than we really are. Any time we have an unrealistic perspective of ourselves, we've lost our basis for healthy relationships because we're not operating from truth.

This also applies to our perspective of each other. When we compare ourselves with other people, we might see them as either better than us or worse than us. If we think they're better than us, we'll relate to them through a lens of our inferiority. If we think they're worse than us, we see them through a lens of our superiority. Both viewpoints rob us of the ability to relate honestly because we are looking through a distorted lens.

Take, for example, the person who ignores their financial situation because they're afraid of the truth. Instead of analyzing their spending and saving habits, they keep shopping and spending and hope for the best. Without knowing the facts about where they stand financially, they'll never be able to deal with the real issues.

Healthy relationships are always based on *truth*. Humility means we can see what's real about ourselves and the other person.

Crazy Love

It's easy to base relationships on how we feel instead of on what's true. When a crazy person has pushed our buttons in the past, we tend to focus on their craziness and assume that we're right. It's uncomfortable to be around their craziness or deal with them, so we take one of two actions:

- We avoid them.
- If we can't avoid them, we try to act like everything's OK so they don't get upset.

But neither option is honest, and both will prolong the pain that comes in the relationship. We can't avoid someone forever, and it's draining to always be pretending.

Kelli thought she was handling her crazy relationships well. Whenever someone was upset with her, she would take the initiative to go to them and find out what she had done wrong. It seemed like an honorable approach because she was trying to make it right. But it was unhealthy because she was doing it out of pride instead of humility.

She always asked for forgiveness and tried to remedy the situation, even when she didn't feel she was in the wrong. It gave her an unconscious sense of pride; she felt like she was better than the other person because she had taken the initiative to fix the relationship. But through that process, Kelli never dealt with the wrong the other person had done and held her anger inside (and felt even more justified because she had controlled that anger). There was no true reconciliation because she hadn't dealt with her anger.

The anger festered and grew, eventually leading to depression. She spent her energy trying to keep people from getting mad at her and never dealt with the underlying issues. She needed to learn to live honestly.

Nobody likes pain. We go to great lengths to avoid it or ignore it. When we feel a physical symptom that concerns us, we might try to ignore it or avoid going to the doctor, hoping it will just go away. We're afraid that the solution might be even more painful than the problem. However, when we ignore the symptoms, we can make the disease worse instead of better.

Relationally healthy people are willing to look honestly at both sides of their relationships so they can correctly diagnose the problems and apply the proper treatment. While this doesn't guarantee a relationship will improve, ignoring the truth will guarantee that it won't.

That's the value of humility—seeing truth as it really is. It has the potential to benefit the other person, but the greater benefit is to ourselves.

What's Love Got to Do with It?

The problem is that we're supposed to love people—even the ones who drive us crazy. We hate hearing that, because it's the last thing we're inclined to do with those people. After all, haven't they made our lives miserable? Why should we even care?

It puts us between a rock and a hard place. The Bible says that love is the greatest commandment of all and that we're even supposed to love our enemies. It's futile trying to exclude our crazy people from that list.

But what does love look like when someone is ruining our lives?

In modern culture, we tend to see love as something we *feel*. In reality, it's something we *do*. Feelings might come and go, but we're still supposed to love. You can't make someone feel something, because feelings aren't something that can be forced. Feelings happen, but we can choose what we do with those feelings.

Let's try it. Right now, I want you to be miserable. Or if you're already miserable, I want you to be ecstatically happy. Go ahead.

How did it go? Not so well, right?

Now let's apply that to the crazy people in your life. I want you to have warm, compassionate feelings toward them. So, that solved everything for you, right?

Not even close.

What then does it mean to love? It means to do things that are in the best interest of the other person. Humility means we need to act not out of selfish motives, but with the other person and their needs in mind.

When couples exchange wedding vows, they promise to love each other. But those vows are really a statement of what they're promising to *do* in the relationship, not what they're going to *feel*. Feelings come and go, and hopefully there will be a lot of positive ones in the relationship. But if the actions they promise at the wedding disappear, so will the feelings.

We've all heard "the Love Chapter" read at weddings (1 Cor. 13:4–8). The description of love includes a lot of statements about actions, not feelings:

- Love is patient (doesn't give up easily)
- Love is kind (treats others with respect, even if it's not returned)
- Love doesn't envy (it is grateful for what one has, without focusing on what one doesn't have)
- Love does not boast, is not proud (doesn't treat others as inferior)
- Love isn't rude (responds to others with integrity)
- Love isn't self-seeking (doesn't put our needs ahead of others')
- Love isn't easily angered (emphasis on "easily")
- Love doesn't keep track of wrongs (doesn't build a case against another person, but handles each situation as it happens)
- Love doesn't delight in evil but rejoices with truth (sees relationships accurately)
- Love never fails (continues to act in the best interests of others)

Think what a marriage would be like if both people actually lived out that description of love. In fact, think what would happen in any relationship if people treated each other that way.

So I Can't Strangle Them?

We have to be honest with our feelings about crazy people. Sometimes that might take the form of "tough love." We can love the crazy people in our lives without handing them the reins of the relationship. We don't need to roll over in submission and always let them have their way. Honestly determining what they need and finding appropriate ways to meet those needs is essential.

Sometimes they might need a carefully crafted confrontation. Other times the situation may call for setting up boundaries to keep the relationship safe for both of us. Most of the time we need to honestly look at our feelings, then take the time to consider the best way to respond instead of reacting in anger.

It might mean staying away from that person while we think through our responses instead of feeling forced to reply in the heat of the situation. For many people, that gives time to develop their thoughts carefully, perhaps even in writing.

It's similar to what we do when we write multiple drafts of a document. We begin by getting everything out on paper, knowing that no one will ever see this rough draft. Then we start revising, editing out the things that don't need to be included and structuring the document for the greatest impact. Finally, we polish the writing so that nothing gets in the way of the point being made in a powerful way.

It takes time to edit our writing, but it produces compelling documents. That's also true in our relationships. When we react immediately to what someone else is saying, it's like showing them the rough draft. They know how we feel, but it often makes the situation worse. There is real value in pulling away, thinking carefully through the most appropriate response (that will give both people what they need), and selecting the best time and situation to deliver those thoughts.

At the same time, we don't have to meet another person's every need. We can only give what we already have. When our emotional tank is on empty, it's not time to pour into someone else's life. It's time to regroup, refresh, and restore our own emotional energy. If I don't take care of me, I won't have anything to give to you.

Tips for Truth

The basis for healthy relationships is seeing ourselves accurately (no better or worse than we really are) and seeing other people accurately.

Instead of interpreting their actions through our emotions, we need to keep our filter of truth functioning properly:

- We need to live outside of ourselves, looking through the eyes of other people (not to agree, necessarily, but to understand).
- We need to remember that people are not accountable to us.
- If we want to change relationships, we need to change ourselves.

11

Key #2—Take Yourself Lightly

You probably know people like this:

- If they won the lottery, they would complain about the taxes they had to pay.
- On a rainy day, they focus on the gray skies instead of getting their lawn watered for free.
- If you compliment them on something they're wearing, they tell you how overweight they feel.
- You call to see how they're doing, and they complain that no one ever calls them.
- When the glass is half-full, they see it as half-empty—and they complain about the color of the glass.

You can count on it. No matter what you say, you know how they'll respond. Some people look at life through a negative lens, which means they see the bad side of any situation. It's become a habit for them, and they don't even realize it.

103

That's a dangerous place to be. People who always look for the negative are targets of crazy people. They're more victimized because they're always looking for the worst in themselves and others. If you ask about the crazy people in their life, you might as well brew a big pot of coffee and pull up a chair for their response. It will take awhile.

Life offers a lot of upsetting situations. But two people can be in the same situation and have totally different responses. Reactive people always focus on the things that are going wrong. Responsive people recognize the power of their choices; they learn to take life lightly and realistically.

That's called *joy*.

What Joy Is—and What It Isn't

Psychologist Tal Ben-Shahar said, "There are two kinds of people in life who don't experience painful emotions such as disappointment or envy or sadness or anxiety: psychopaths and the dead."[1] Since you're reading this book, you're probably not in either category. We want a happy life; but if we assume that means having uninterrupted positive emotions, we're setting ourselves up for disappointment.

Every situation has two sides: negative and positive.

- It was a great vacation, but it's time to go back to work.
- The dinner party was a success, but the kitchen is in shambles.
- You love your new car, but you have to make the payments each month.
- You have crazy people in your life, but you have sane ones as well.

A healthy person's life is characterized by *joy*. That might seem unrealistic, considering the people who are in our lives. But joy comes from inside us, not from outside. Joy is something that comes into our lives when we replace our negative lens with a bigger perspective of truth. That doesn't mean everything will suddenly be perfect; it just means we'll see people and situations as they really are.

When our kids were little, we often played a game around the dinner table we called "Bright Side." Anytime someone shared something painful that happened during their day, they would also have to share something positive that happened. They might be in a bad mood and not feel like going there, but the exercise almost always lifted their spirits before we were done. It was a reminder that life is not entirely made up of bad experiences and people; it also includes good ones. It's important to see both sides. The truth is not that the glass is half-full or half-empty; it's that the glass has water in it. Some of it is gone and some of it is left. That's seeing things realistically.

Rainbows in Your Mud Puddles

Years ago, when video cameras first became popular for home use, a friend purchased one. She used it constantly. When her kids had birthday parties, she recorded every minute. She followed the kids around, trying to capture each moment for the future.

But it always seemed like she was so busy recording the moments that she became an observer instead of a participant. She missed the moments. Later, she could review the tape and see her children playing, but she would never see herself playing with them.

Joyful people are participants. They don't miss the moments. They turn moments into memories.

My tendency in most situations is to be thinking about what I'm going to do or say next instead of enjoying the moment. However, I've been learning to build memories by being fully engaged in what I'm doing. It's not natural, but it's entirely possible. The more engaged I am in what's happening around me, whether positive or negative, the greater the memories are in the future.

It takes practice. As I approach each conversation, I have to remind myself to be completely focused on that person and block the random thoughts that distract me. By doing so, each event I'm part of becomes much richer and builds richer memories.

Negative people see their lives as a series of crises, interrupted occasionally by joyful moments. What if we reversed it, seeing life as positive but interrupted by occasional speed bumps? Both the positive and negative moments are real; it's simply a matter of where we put our focus.

On a clear night we look up and see a full moon and a sky filled with stars. The beauty of that scene can take our breath away. The darkness is real and might take up the majority of the sky. But when we look at the stars or the moon, we don't notice the darkness; it only provides contrast so we can focus on the brilliance of the night sky.

That's the way we can look at life. The dark is there, but it doesn't have to be our primary focus. We can consciously focus on the light, letting the darkness provide the contrast to bring richness to each moment.

It's a realistic approach to life based on truth.

Choosing Our Focus

Having a "light" approach to life is a conscious choice. Other people and circumstances try to drag us down. We have to *choose* to see life differently. It's not a choice based on positive self-talk or affirmations; it's a choice based on reality.

Emotional control is determined by where we put our focus. We can choose to focus on one of three things:

1. Crazy people
2. Ourselves
3. Truth

Crazy People

Crazy people can ruin our lives if we put our focus on them and their behavior. Yes, they are still going to be in our lives, and they'll probably continue trying to push our buttons. But if we put too much energy and focus on them, they'll be in control of our emotions. We'll become dominated by their choices and behaviors.

Ourselves

This is a better choice of where to direct our energy, because we take personal responsibility for what happens to us instead of letting other people control our emotions. The downside is that when we're feeling victimized, focusing on ourselves can mean that we're focusing on what's wrong instead of what's right and possible. We're looking at what's dark rather than what's bright.

Truth

Truth is like the US Constitution. When people want to know if something is right or wrong, they go to court. At the highest level, the Supreme Court holds each case up to the Constitution to determine if it's "constitutional." It shouldn't matter whether the justices like the outcome or not. The Constitution isn't evaluated by the case; the case is evaluated by the Constitution.

Focusing on what's true in every relationship and every situation doesn't mean life will be perfect. But when we see things accurately, we can choose accurate responses. The only way we know we're making good choices is if they're based on truth.

In our relationships, focusing on what is true and accurate can change the way we feel. How do we determine what is true? Consider these perspectives we can focus on:

- What is it about the crazy person's words, attitude, or behavior that pushes our buttons? What doesn't push those buttons?
- What good things are happening in our life? Can we be grateful for those things?
- What things can we do something about? What can we *not* do anything about?
- What am I feeling? How accurate are those emotions?

Our actions come from our feelings, which come from our thoughts, which come from our inputs. If we make sure the inputs are accurate, we'll think clearly. Clear thinking leads to control of our emotions, which results in appropriate choices.

The Problem with Mental Multitasking

In a fast-paced society, most people have learned to multitask as a way of getting more done. On the surface, it seems beneficial, because we seem to be accomplishing two things at once. It's common to see someone checking email while on the phone, making a grocery list while coordinating schedules with the kids, or texting while driving. But often we miss some critical detail from a phone call and have to call back, or we leave something off the grocery list and have to make a return trip to the store.

Studies have shown that our minds can only do one thing at a time. When we're multitasking, our mind is actually switching back and forth rapidly between the two activities, slowing down the entire process. Multitasking actually takes more time and mental energy and causes a higher level of stress than if we had a single focus for each activity.

Our minds will always be focused on something. When we've gotten used to focusing on what our crazy person does, we can't just stop thinking about it. Negative thoughts seem to follow the course of least resistance. When our minds go into neutral, they automatically tend to flow toward our normal thinking patterns, whether negative or positive. If we try to stop thinking about something, it creates a vacuum—and our minds go right back to what we were just thinking about. It seems like there's no escape.

But that brain function is also the solution. We can't simply try to stop thinking about the negative people and situations in our lives. We have to *replace* those thoughts, consciously choosing other things to fill our minds with. At first the negative thoughts will try to sneak back in because they've been there for so long. But when that happens, it can become the trigger to again fill our minds with truth.

Trying to think of new responses when we're in the middle of the emotion is like signing up for swimming lessons when the boat is sinking. It's something we need to think through before the emotion hits us.

Step 1: Write down all the negative thoughts that go through our minds regarding that person or situation.

- They said I was annoying and that everyone else thinks so too. I guess I am. I wonder who else feels that way?
- Since we're related, there's nothing I can do.
- That person has it in for me.
- They're making my life miserable.

Step 2: Determine what's true about each of those items, and put them in writing.

- Maybe they think I'm annoying, but no one else has given me reason to believe that. I need to focus on them, and not assume things about others.
- We're related, but I don't have to be a victim. I can't force them to change, but I can influence them.
- It feels like they have it in for me, but it probably has more to do with the way they handle all their relationships. It feels personal, but they're probably not targeting me.
- They can't *make* my life miserable; I'm allowing it. I know who I am and where my value is, no matter what they say. I can set boundaries that protect me from their words and actions.

Step 3: When we find ourselves stuck in negative thought patterns, it becomes a trigger to review the things we know to be true, what we can control, and what we can't control.

As soon as we realize where our thoughts have taken us, we can stop and say, "Wait a minute. I'm letting that person control my emotions. Let me review what I know to be true: I'm a good person; my value doesn't come from what they think; I have people who care deeply about me; I can choose how I respond; I have talents and skills . . ."

Step 4: Upon waking each morning, we can train ourselves to think of five things we're grateful for before getting out of bed to set the right tone for the day. At night, we can repeat the process right before going to sleep.

Bottom line: It's possible to learn to think differently, replacing negative thought patterns with positive ones. When we do that, we have a realistic chance of developing a new lens through which we see life: a lens of *joy*.

Points for Perspective

Tony Snow, former press secretary for President George W. Bush, died of cancer at the age of fifty-three. He wrote, "We all want lives of simple, predictable ease—smooth, even trails as far as the eye can see. *But God likes to go off-road.*"[2]

We like to go off-roading when it's fun and safe, but not when it becomes painful or dangerous. So, how can we live with joy?

By choosing where we put our focus.

- The darkness is real, but the light is just as real.
- The negative is real, but the positive is just as real.
- The pain is real, but healing is just as real.

We don't want our lives to be defined by the craziness of others, letting them hold our emotions hostage. Even if we've felt victimized by our upbringing, our circumstances, life events, or crazy people, we can choose where to put our focus.

We can choose joy.

12

Key #3—Don't Sweat the Wrong Stuff

Richard Carlson wrote a bestselling book a number of years ago titled *Don't Sweat the Small Stuff*. The concept was simple: put your energy into the big things that really matter rather than the things that don't. It's a great concept and helped people sort through the urgent things in life that weren't so important.[1]

If I were rewriting the book, I would call it *Don't Sweat the Wrong Stuff*. It's a slight adjustment to the concept, because I've found that sometimes the small stuff *is* important, while less valuable things often take huge amounts of time and energy.

There have been times when I've been on a long walk or run and gotten a tiny pebble in my shoe. Sometimes it's barely the size of a large grain of sand, so I try to ignore it. In the big picture of things, it's not that important and I won't die from it. But if don't stop and take care of it, it's all I can think about. If I wait too long, it begins to irritate my foot until it becomes painful.

If you've ever gotten a splinter or had a sliver of corn on the cob stuck between your teeth, you know how irritating it can be. Focusing on it is irresistible, and all we can think about is getting it out. As small as it is, it impacts our performance until it's taken care of.

Small things can be important, and big things can be meaningless. People who have healthy relationships are more concerned with value than size. They've learned to discern which things are worth fighting for and which things to ignore. They've learned to pick their battles.

Fighting the Right Battles

A lot of people get upset at everything that happens around them. They're on a lifelong quest to see the negative in everything, and they appoint themselves the caretaker of everyone else's behavior. That perspective keeps them steeped in drama.

We observe those people, see their pain, and decide what they should do. After all, we know what solutions have worked for us; we assume those solutions will work for them as well. If they do what we did, they'll feel better.

But fixing others isn't our responsibility. We're choosing the *wrong stuff* when we try. We're only responsible for our own choices and actions. In relationships, the "wrong stuff" is anything that is the responsibility of another person.

When my wife and I bought our first house back in the 1980s, we had a neighbor who didn't take the greatest care of his lawn. He would mow it but never edge it. So it always looked scraggly and unkempt creeping over the sidewalk. We never talked about it, but I always thought it needed to be done.

One morning, as I was mowing and edging my lawn, I took the edger over to his lawn and trimmed against his sidewalk. It only took about ninety seconds, and looked great after I swept up the debris. I really thought I was helping him, and I expected him to be excited. But he never mentioned it. That surprised me because I had hoped he would be grateful. Looking back, I realize how it might have seemed like I was judging him by doing that. It really wasn't my responsibility, but I had taken it on myself and assumed what he wanted and needed.

That's the wrong stuff—taking upon myself the responsibilities of others. If we're going to have healthy relationships, we need to determine what we're responsible for, what we're not responsible for, and what's important.

The more we focus on our own responsibilities instead of trying to fix everyone else, the more we'll be in charge of our own emotions. Contentment in life doesn't come from the absence of conflict; it comes from not giving away our emotional control to the demands of other people. We learn how to be independent in our choices instead of being dependent on what other people do or think.

Does that mean that crazy people will still cause us pain? Of course, because we're human. It's going to hurt if you hit me, and I may have pain and bruising for a long time. But if I focus my energy on anger and revenge, I'm choosing to let you control my emotions. It's become all about you.

I watched a movie once where one man stabbed another, then ran away. The wound was serious but not life-threatening if the victim could receive medical attention. But that injured person was so angry with the attacker that he began chasing him. Block after block he ran, trying to catch up with the man and take revenge. Because of blood loss, he grew weaker and weaker until his run turned into a walk, then a crawl, and he finally died on the sidewalk.

That's what happens when we keep our focus on the person who caused us the injury. Even though I feel angry, I need to step back and determine how I should respond. Should I go after you in anger and look for revenge, or should I seek medical attention? It's like the safety announcements on airlines where we're told to put on our own oxygen mask before helping our kids. It might sound cruel, but if we don't take care of ourselves first, our children won't get what they need to survive.

That's the right stuff. When crazy people wound us, we need "medical attention." We need to take care of ourselves first and make sure we're thinking accurately and responding correctly. Only then are we able to determine the best way to respond to the person who hurt us.

We can't fix everyone who causes us pain. If it's an important relationship, we might be able to make restoration in the future. But many circumstances will involve setting up appropriate boundaries to keep from being a victim.

Tina loves her mother-in-law, but she drops in unexpectedly several times a week. Her husband, Richard, doesn't like it either but feels guilty confronting his mother. If they ignore the situation, they allow themselves to be manipulated by her lack of sensitivity. Setting boundaries means that the two of them would talk through what their needs are as a couple, then determine what a healthy relationship with his mother would look like. They will need to have the tough conversation with her, expressing their care for her and their desire to see her while setting the parameters for their relationship. It might not be comfortable, but it sets boundaries to protect their relationship.

The Perspective of Contentment

No one wants to be a victim. We don't want other people bringing chaos into our lives, because it pulls us away from our set point. When we get too far from that set point, everything inside us clamors to get back to that place of calm and comfort.

We might assume that contentment means smooth sailing in everything we do, that we'll be at our set point and nobody will be messing up our lives. However, it's unrealistic to think that we'll be free from conflict in this life.

But it's possible to have serenity even in the midst of conflict. The Bible has over 250 references suggesting that contentment can be a reality. It doesn't eliminate pain, but it's something we can experience no matter what happens around us.

Sound impossible? Especially when you've felt trapped by the drama that others have brought into your life for so long?

The more we pick the right battles and learn to focus on the right stuff instead of the wrong stuff, the better chance we have of staying closer to our set point. It doesn't happen automatically. Learning where to put our focus is a process that takes action on our part.

New Thinking for a New Attitude

The key to being in control of our emotions is to work on our thinking patterns. Our thoughts determine our feelings. If we want different feelings, we need different thoughts. What should we think about?

1. We can choose not to worry. When we worry, it paralyzes us from taking action. Focusing on what we know is true in a situation or relationship takes our mind off the situation and onto the solution.
2. We can focus on things that are positive, seeing what's right about a relationship instead of just what's wrong.
3. We can control our emotions toward the other person instead of letting them be the captain of our feelings.

Over time, optimism begins to replace concern. The right stuff replaces the wrong stuff.

Inputs Produce Outputs

There is a logical assumption that goes with this. By choosing good things to focus on, it implies that we're supposed to consciously *not* focus on bad things. That's tough to do when we're surrounded by negative inputs in the media, in our relationships, and in the filters of other people. But our thoughts come from our inputs. That's why we need to be aware of what we allow to come into our minds.

115

Several years ago, I became aware of my inputs and what they were producing in my life. I realized that my mental inputs come primarily from sight and sound. So I decided to keep track of both.

Most mornings, I would start the day by reading the newspaper. Once I was in my car, I would listen to the news or local radio hosts. As soon as I sat down at my computer I would check my email. By midmorning, I usually felt overwhelmed and agitated about my day. Throughout the day I would have a number of conversations, but I wasn't very discerning about whether those people were positive or negative forces in my life. I listened to talk radio in the car on my way home and was too burned out to have meaningful conversation with my family. It felt like I was at the mercy of everyone else in my life.

So my day was filled with inputs about negative things that were happening around the world, opinions of angry people, electronic demands from dozens of people in my world, and conversations with people who had negative stories or gossip to share. I couldn't find much that would be considered life-giving.

And I wondered why I always felt grumpy!

I made some simple changes in those inputs, and the results were dramatic:

- I dropped my subscription to the newspaper and read one chapter in a good book each morning: sometimes fiction, sometimes nonfiction, often the biblical book of Proverbs.

- In the car, I tried listening to music or simply leaving the radio off. I would listen to the headlines at the top of the hour for two minutes to get the top stories on my way home, then turn the radio off.

- I made a simple adjustment in my computer settings to bring my calendar up before my email, so I could focus on my own priorities before the urgencies of others.

- I sought out the most positive people in my day and intentionally spent time with them.

- I thinned out my Facebook friends, going for quality over quantity.
- I quit checking my email after dinner, leaving the evening free to focus on things that mattered more. I figured that if it was a real emergency, they wouldn't email. (I don't get too many emails that say, "I'm choking" . . .)

It wasn't long before I began to feel differently. I was operating on a new type of fuel and was able to perform at a much higher level. My improved inputs dramatically impacted my outputs.

Try this exercise: all day tomorrow, from the time you get up until the time you go to bed, observe the things that you allow into your mind. When you read the paper or watch the news, notice the balance between positive and negative inputs. Observe the people you spend time with during the day and analyze their conversations. Listen to your own perspective on the crazy people in your life.

At the end of the day, evaluate the inputs you had. How many of them would fit the category of being positive and encouraging, and how many forced you to focus on everything that's wrong? Then think about the emotions you felt during the day. Were they positive or negative?

There is a direct correlation between the things we think about (our inputs) and the emotions we have (our outputs). Bad inputs, bad emotions. Good inputs, good emotions. Whenever we feel like crazy people are controlling our lives and we can't seem to escape our feelings, we need to check our inputs.

Right-Side Up Thinking

I have a telescope on my patio. Usually I use it for studying the moon, planets, or stars, but sometimes I focus on the hills that are miles in the distance. Part of those hills is covered with housing developments, while the rest is simply scenic.

My telescope has two lenses. The first one gives me a pretty good view of things in the distance. I get an accurate picture and am able to distinguish individual houses, trees, and landmarks. If I look carefully, I can even see cars and trucks traveling on distant streets.

The second lens is much stronger than the first. With it, I can focus on the same scenery but see it in greater detail. By keeping the telescope steady, I can actually see blurry images of people walking down the street, even though they are miles away.

But there's a problem with that second lens: it turns everything upside down. That's not a problem when I'm looking at the sky. But when I'm looking at the landscape, I'm seeing everything from the wrong perspective.

The problem isn't with the people I'm seeing; it's with my lens. Our tendency is to look through our upside-down lenses and assume that what we see is reality. In my quest to see things in closer detail, I sacrifice the broader perspective that shows me what is real.

In relationships we think, "Those people are crazy—they're upside-down." It's important to know that by ourselves we have only the upside-down lens, which distorts the reality of relationships. The other lens is the lens of truth. We might not see as much detail with it, but we will see the crazy people in our lives right-side up. Only through that truth lens will we see the bigger picture and have a credible claim to contentment in our lives.

How do we keep positive perspective in the tough situations?

- Become a connoisseur of truth.
- Surround yourself with people who build positively into your life.
- Choose your inputs carefully.
- Set appropriate physical and emotional boundaries for the crazy people.
- Don't try to fix everyone else.
- Don't sweat the wrong stuff.

Dr. Larry Poland of Mastermedia International, a nonprofit ministry to cultural influencers in Hollywood, often talks about how Christians try to repair the moral decay in the media by boycotting, writing letters, and protesting. Though well-intentioned, those techniques usually cause media leaders to see Christians as people who hate them and only care about having them clean up their act. Dr. Poland practices a different perspective on being "fishers of men." He says, "It's our job to catch them; it's God's job to clean them."

Contentment comes when we know what things we're responsible for and which ones we should let go. When we base our relationships on what is accurate and real, we can find light in the darkest night.

Mood Mastery

Try this exercise; all it takes is asking yourself two questions. One: What's the situation? (Describe.) *My boss is crazy. He never gives me any encouragement or catches me doing anything right, and is quick to point out my mistakes. I like the work I do, and I'm good at it. But I hate going to work because his attitude just ruins everything.*

Two: What's bugging me about it? List every aspect that concerns you in the appropriate column:

Things I can't do anything about	Things I *can* do something about
My boss's personality	How I perform my work
My boss's management style	How I choose to relate to my boss
My boss's choices	How I choose to respond when my boss is unreasonable
My boss's priorities	My conversations with other people about my boss
How my boss sees his job and his responsibilities	The value I can bring to my boss as I grow in my skills
	What I know to be true about myself and my work
↓	↓
Action	**Action**
If it's in this column, *don't* put any energy here	If it's in this column, *put* your energy here

In other words:

What *can* I control? *Me—my choices and attitudes*

What can I *not* control? Everything else—including my boss.

13

Key #4—Don't Rush Growth

When my wife and I were first married, we lived in a tiny, old cottage in Redondo Beach, California. We painted the house, put in a lawn, and planted flowers. The soil was rich and loamy, and everything we planted flourished. We assumed it was because we were such good gardeners.

Two years later, we moved to Phoenix, Arizona. We moved into a new home in the desert and assumed our gardening skills would transfer there. But the clay soil was like concrete. I had to buy a pick just to break up the ground enough to plant snapdragons (they died). Our intentions were good, but we knew nothing about growing things in the desert. We needed help.

"Citrus," the nurseryman said, "grows great in Arizona." So we bought an orange tree, a lemon tree, and a grapefruit tree. We dug the holes, added the mulch and nutrients, and planted the trees. We watered them and waited, anticipating the day when we would serve fresh-picked fruit to friends on our patio for breakfast.

The trees grew well, but there wasn't any fruit. The same thing happened the next year. We had lush foliage but nothing to show for all our work. So we went back to the nursery for advice.

"Time," the nurseryman said. "It can take three years for fruit to appear on newly planted citrus trees in Arizona." That wasn't the answer I was hoping for, but it gave me hope. That next year, we had one small orange, a couple of anorexic lemons, and one Texas-sized grapefruit. But the following year, the sweet smell of citrus blossoms gave way to dozens of fruit on each tree.

During those initial years, I really wanted the fruit and it was hard to wait. I could have gone to the grocery store and purchased a bag of oranges, a bag of lemons, some grapefruit, and a roll of tape, and just taped the fruit onto the trees. Then I could honestly say there was fruit on my trees. But I would be rushing the end result, which would have defeated the purpose of the tree.

Trees aren't supposed to *display* fruit; they're supposed to *produce* it. As much as I wanted to see results, I knew that I had to wait. The tree had to become healthy and mature before it could produce the fruit, and that takes time.

That's true in our relationships as well. We would love to see people "shape up" and fix the problems in their lives right away. But it takes time for real change to take place, if it happens at all. To keep from being emotionally trapped and frustrated by other people's lack of progress, we need to accept the reality that growth and healing often take time.

Comedian Bob Newhart once did a classic routine where he played the part of a psychologist. Every time the woman in his office began describing her symptoms and phobias, Newhart would yell, "Stop it!" That was his solution to every problem: "Just stop it!"

We love watching that in a comedy routine, but it's probably because we recognize that tendency in our own lives. We see someone trapped in a behavior that's causing pain for themselves and everyone around them, and we think, "Why can't they just see what they're doing and STOP IT?"

But we also know from personal experience that it's almost impossible to just stop something that has been a pattern in our lives for years. Once a pattern has taken root in our lives, it's like yanking a fifty-year-old oak tree out of the ground. It's possible, but it takes time and usually involves dealing with one root at a time.

Addicted to Hurry

English prime minister Margaret Thatcher once said, "I am extraordinarily patient, provided I get my own way in the end." We've heard that patience is a virtue, but it's tough in a microwave society where we've become used to quick solutions. If someone hesitates for one second when the traffic light turns green, people begin to honk. When a shopper in the grocery store checkout is sorting through their coins one penny at a time to make exact change, we're ready to call security. If a website doesn't load within a second or two, we get frustrated and move to a different site.

I was a college professor when personal computers first came onto the scene. The faculty at our school attended four days of training on how to use computers. The first program they demonstrated was a simple calculator that would add, subtract, multiply, and divide. But the program was on a cassette tape, and we had to press "play" to load the program onto the computer. It took about six minutes to load, but that didn't bother us since we were focused on what we could do once it was done.

Can you imagine waiting six minutes for a program to load on your computer today?

Maybe that's why we tend to be impatient with our relationships. We're surrounded by instant everything, and we want instant solutions from the craziness people bring into our lives. We feel like they've taken residence in a little corner of our lives, and we're not sure how to move them out.

We've heard that patience is a virtue, but we assume that the person who said that was an only child raised by hyenas. If patience is such a good thing, then why is it so hard to exercise when we're surrounded by craziness?

Part of it is our environment. When we're immersed in a culture of instant gratification, patience isn't our default setting. We've trained it right out of our lives. As a result, we're more easily irritated when people don't change. Often, people *do* change, but it doesn't happen overnight. One area of their life improves, but we focus on the many areas that still produce pain. We forget that genuine change takes time.

The Value of Time

Business classes often discuss two principles of economics:

1. The three elements you have to work with are quality, price, and convenience.
2. You can pick any two, but not all three.

For example, a corner convenience store usually offers name-brand products (quality) and easy parking (convenience)—but you'll pay a lot more for those items (price). A mega-warehouse store offers top quality and great prices, but you'll park farther away and stand in long lines (convenience). There are also stores that are known for extremely low prices and convenient access, but you'll sacrifice quality.

That's similar to how relationships work. We meet people at a wedding or other social event (convenient) and make a brief connection with them (time), but we haven't yet developed the kind of friendship where we share our deepest feelings (quality). Other people have become close friends (quality) because we've lived through life events together over the years (time); but they have moved out of the area, so it takes a concentrated effort to maintain that friendship (convenience).

Then there are those people who drive us crazy. If they're a casual acquaintance, it's easy to blow them off and avoid them so they don't irritate us. But when it's a family member whom we can't avoid, it adds another dimension. It might be someone we really care about, but we don't honestly express our feelings because we're afraid of their reactions. We would love to see them change, but it seems like it will take forever (if it happens at all) and we lose hope.

It's true that they might never change. But even if they do, it won't happen immediately. Quality relationships are built over time, not overnight. The more we can accept that reality, the less frustration we'll feel.

I recently read about a master craftsman who builds violins for a living. He is meticulous about quality, but convenience goes out the window. Working full-time, he only makes one violin every nine months. But people pay between $80,000 and $100,000 for that violin when he's finished.

People who have learned to handle the craziness of others have developed the character quality of patience, knowing they can't rush growth.

The Secret of Patience

When people cut us off in traffic, we usually assume that they're incompetent, arrogant knuckleheads who think they own the road. We make character judgments about them and feel justified in our reaction. We *know* they're crazy. But we've cut others off accidently because we weren't paying attention. It wasn't intentional; it was a mistake. Probably.

We don't really know what's going through another person's mind, even though we're convinced that we do. A person who possesses patience might still get upset when someone cuts her off. But she has learned not to interpret the other driver's motives. The other person might have done it on purpose or might have made a mistake. Neither one makes it any better, but a patient person doesn't give away the control of her emotions to the other person by stewing about it the rest of the day.

It all goes back to *truth*. If we know what's true in a situation (i.e., another person's motives), we can make accurate decisions about how we should respond. If we don't know what's true, we have only our assumptions. If our assumptions are wrong, our interpretation is wrong and our responses will be inappropriate. With inappropriate responses, we'll never be able to respond with patience.

Patience doesn't mean sitting and waiting for another person to change. It doesn't mean we passively allow others to abuse us, and it doesn't mean every encounter with them will be comfortable. Patience is what develops inside of us *between* those encounters. It's the characteristic that helps us stay strong when things are tough over the long haul.

So, where do we get patience if we don't have it? People often joke that we shouldn't pray for patience because God will bring crazy people into our lives to teach it to us. I don't think that's very good theology, but it makes an interesting point.

Like any other positive trait, patience is something that builds into our lives over time. Just as muscles grow through repeated exercise, patience grows as we repeatedly practice responding to others in healthy ways.

If you brush your teeth twice a day, two minutes each time, it adds up to over twenty-four hours at the end of a year. What if you decided to be more efficient and do it all at once? Take the day off work, start at midnight, and brush for the next twenty-four hours straight. You wouldn't have to brush your teeth for an entire year!

The same thing is true of patience. We can't get a giant dose of it and expect it to last all year. It's something that develops in us as we choose the appropriate response in each situation we encounter.

Learn from Looking Inward

Suppose that ten years ago you had written down what you expected to be like today; not about your possessions and successes, but about your character, attitudes, and actions. Looking at who you are today, how do you feel about the progress you've made? Are you where you thought you would be? Are your attitudes and integrity what you had hoped for?

Most of us would say, "I'm still in process. Yes, I'm doing better, but I have a long way to go." Patience is when we focus on the process rather than the lack of results. It's learning to give ourselves a break for not being perfect.

That's what needs to happen in our relationships with others. Learning patience means seeing through the lens of truth:

- Change takes time.
- It's not our job to fix others, and we'll be frustrated if we count on doing so.
- Everyone is in process.
- Each person changes on a unique timetable, not according to our schedule.

A good example is someone who has suffered a brain injury. Casual observers notice how unresponsive the person is and how little they can do. A close family member sees that reality but also becomes excited at the smallest sign of progress, such as the squeeze of a hand. They're improving, but it doesn't happen overnight.

Patience allows us to let people change at their own pace. Without it, we're putting all of our hope in future progress instead of living in present reality.

14

Key #5—Live Through the Lens of Kindness

Would you rather be kind or successful?

- If a person watches an hour of news and tries to describe the condition of the world, "kindness" probably won't be part of that description.
- Studies show that trust in government and organizational leadership is at an all-time low.
- Reality shows build their audience by revealing the dishonest tactics people use to sabotage others, while faking kindness to win their trust.
- When political and economic fortunes change, survival seems to focus on a person's ability to outwit, outplay, and outlast others.

Kindness is seen as irrelevant, or it's just something you do to gain an advantage over others.

People buy books about how to be healthy, wealthy, popular, and balanced. But few people are rushing out to buy books on how to be kind. In our competitive world, we seem to think kindness would keep us from achieving greatness. When we think of successful people, kindness isn't the first word that comes to mind.

We might admit that kindness is a good virtue, and we appreciate those few people in our lives who are characterized by it. But deep inside, we might actually see it as a weakness rather than a strength.

I remember a sermon once where the pastor said, "No one wants to have 'They were nice' written on their tombstone." The implication is that if someone was known for being nice, they didn't accomplish anything in life.

In that context, being *kind* seems to be taking a step backward. It feels like weakness—like subduing the passion and quenching the fire that drives us. People assume that being kind means rolling over and always being nonconfrontational. Those with an outgoing temperament feel as if they have to give up their natural personality to become something they're not. Those with quieter personalities often use kindness to justify not striving for more.

Kindness is universally understood to be a virtue. But in a success-driven culture, few people go out of their way to make it part of their life. They see it as optional, like seat warmers in a new car: nice, but not essential.

But the reason isn't because kindness is old-fashioned; it's misunderstood. Kindness is not just gentleness or niceness; it's a key element in a successful life. Kindness is a vital part of strength.

The Strength of Kindness

Kindness and strength are not mutually exclusive. Strength without kindness is abusive. Kindness without strength is impotent. Only when both are used together will we make a true impact on the lives of others.

When dealing with the crazy people in our lives, we fear that any display of kindness will be seen as a weak spot that invites attack. But only strong people can be truly kind. Kindness becomes one of the characteristics that enable us to deal effectively with others.

My granddaughters, ages four and six, often surprise me with their kindness for each other. They still fight like most kids, but they seem to have a "sixth sense" about times when the other needs a gentle touch. I've seen Averie spend her own money to buy a treat for her younger sister, Elena, because she knows what it would mean to her. Elena is often the first to share a favorite dessert with her sister just to be kind. The more they demonstrate kindness, the greater the bond develops between them.

Think about how we feel when someone demonstrates kindness to us. We don't just notice the act of kindness; we feel differently about that person, period. Kindness is an emotional handshake that builds trust between two people.

The results become even more obvious when someone demonstrates kindness to their enemy. One person is expecting criticism or judgment from another but receives kindness instead. Even when there is strong disagreement or injury, it's hard to ignore the fact that they were treated with respect and kindness, minimizing the offense.

A common fear is that we'll have to give up our personality in order to be kind. We want to be fully engaged in life, and we don't want to pretend to be something we're not. We fear living our lives with the directive to "be kind" lurking in the background, suggesting that we need to tone our personalities down a notch. We feel like we're supposed to paint our lives beige.

Kindness isn't a replacement for personality; it's a catalyst that makes our personality more effective. Adding salt to food doesn't replace the food, it enhances the natural flavor. Kindness brings out the richness in relationships.

The Science of Kindness

Kindness helps us become effective in our daily life and relationships. Regardless of a person's personality, gender, or age, kindness is a key to success in every area of life. It provides the solution for negotiating the lack of trust in our society. Rather than a gimmick for survival, it becomes the means for impacting the lives of others, a catalyst for change in the world.

We don't become kind by doing kind things for others. We do kind things for others because we're kind.

It seems that kind people live longer, are more popular, more productive, happier, and have greater business success than others. Kindness is more than a virtue; it provides real-world benefits for both the giver and the receiver.

We've often heard the phrase "Nice guys finish last." But after spending over two decades in the corporate world, I've found the opposite is more often true. There are tyrants who have bullied their way to the top, but their employees usually are much less loyal, engaged, and excited about being part of the company. They have used the appearance of kindness as a gimmick to gain compliance from their followers, but it results in low trust within the organization.

I've found that the phrase "Cream rises to the top" is more accurate. Many of the executives I've worked with in major corporations and organizations made it to the top by developing real relationships with the people around them on the way up. Starting at the bottom, they genuinely cared about the people around them. Instead of manipulating for their own advantage, they built trust at that level and their influence began to grow as they rose through the ranks.

When someone treats us with kindness, it catches us off guard because it happens so rarely. It makes us want to connect with that person, and we find ourselves being kind in return.

The same is true for an unkind person. When they treat us unkindly, it makes us want to avoid them. We don't trust them and are always suspicious of their actions and motives.

What if we short-circuited the process by being kind to a person who was unkind? There are no guarantees of how they might respond, but it would change the dynamics in the relationship. It's not about being kind so the other person will change. It's about being kind because it's *right*.

It's the Golden Rule: "Do unto others as you would have them do unto you."

Being kind to the unkind is the opposite of being manipulative. True kindness isn't a technique we use to change someone else. It's a character trait that causes us to care for others no matter what they do or say. It doesn't mean we have to be outgoing and friendly to a crazy person when they have hurt us. It just means we treat them with respect and kindness as a person. It brings meaning to the verse, "Love your enemies" (Matt. 5:44).

Terry was the new guy in his office, hiring on less than three months past. Most of the other salespeople treated him well, but Bill seemed to have it in for him. Bill had been there longer than anyone else and was always the top salesperson. He was the best; he knew it, and he made sure everyone else knew it. No one knew for sure whether it was arrogance or insecurity that made him attack Terry so often, pointing out that the new guy just didn't have what it took to be successful. Bill was sarcastic to Terry's face and demeaning behind his back.

Terry wasn't one to be pushed around. He didn't fight back or use the same tactics that Bill did; instead, he consistently treated Bill with kindness. Terry protected himself by not spending much time around Bill, although he did his best to make every encounter positive. To Bill's face, he tried to affirm him as a person as well as for his competence. He did the same thing behind Bill's back. When everyone else was calling Bill a jerk, Terry focused on his strengths. He knew there was more than what was on the surface, because people don't act the way Bill did without something painful in their past fueling their behavior.

The turning point came when Terry was working a huge account that would have given him thousands of dollars in commission. He knew that Bill would be a better fit for the client and made arrangements with the client for Bill to take his place. It was a simple act of kindness that spoke volumes.

Bill and Terry will never be best friends, and Bill is still seen by others as a jerk. An unspoken respect grew between Bill and Terry. Bill never says anything positive about Terry, but he also doesn't say anything negative. Terry chose genuine kindness, and Bill found it irresistible. It hasn't changed Bill's life, but it has changed their relationship.

Crazy Kindness

When crazy people wrap their tentacles around our lives, we can't pretend everything is OK in order to keep them happy. There is an appropriate time, place, and need for confrontation. But we ought to do it with a focus on the interests of other people as well as our own interests.

You might be asking, "So, do I have to be kind to a jerk?"

It's natural to feel more positive toward some people than others. We'll be closer to some people and not as close to others. When we're angry with someone or they have hurt us, kindness isn't the first response we think of. But if we define kindness correctly, it can be a genuine part of every relationship—even the toughest ones. It doesn't mean we ignore the situation; it means we look at the other person and what they're doing through more understanding eyes.

When we have nothing left to give because hurtful things have sucked us dry, it's OK. Even in the midst of pain, we can choose kindness as an appropriate and healthy response—whether we're dealing with crazy people, whiny kids, rebellious teens, elderly relatives suffering from dementia, or even a puppy who chews the cover off our favorite book.

The Dream of Kindness

What would the world be like if everyone practiced kindness, even toward people they disagreed with? What would happen to wars, politics, governments, families, and churches? What if people had to take a course on kindness before appearing in a reality television show?

John Donne once said, "No man is an island."[1] Like the expanding ripple that spreads across a pond when a pebble is tossed in, one person's kindness can have that effect—in another person's life, as well as impacting society as a whole.

Kindness is contagious. It's an antacid for living in a toxic world. It's the tool God has given us to change the world by influencing others—one heart at a time.

15

Key #6—Base Your Choices on Integrity, Not Convenience

Several times each year, I conduct seminars at the major movie studios in Hollywood. My favorite part of the day is the lunch hour, when I dismiss the class and take a walk through the studio lots where hundreds of movies have been filmed over the years. It's always fun to walk down the "streets" I recognize from some of my favorite TV shows and films.

On the screen, it looks like you're walking through the downtown area of a major city. The close-up view in person reveals well-designed storefronts and buildings with nothing behind them except the scaffolding that holds them up. They look real but they're hollow inside, nothing but a façade.

The entertainment industry is built on make-believe. Actors and actresses are real people pretending to be someone else, saying words that someone else gave them in buildings that don't really exist. Millions of us spend millions of hours and billions of dollars watching the fantasy, knowing it's not real but engaging with the characters as if we've known them for years.

I'm not criticizing the industry any more than I would criticize fiction books. We all love a good story. But it becomes a problem when our relationships are based on "characters" that aren't what they seem, pretending to be one way while the reality is totally different. When relationships are built around surface characteristics instead of internal character, there is no hope for handling crazy people in a healthy way.

We need a good dose of *integrity*.

The Impact of Integrity

In the past, most people shared a common definition of what it meant to have integrity: you were honest, and you could be trusted. You could be counted on to tell the truth. If you didn't have integrity, you were a liar.

But several decades ago, a "new" version of integrity became popular, called "situational ethics." That meant we handled any situation based on what was convenient for us. If telling the truth would be uncomfortable or embarrassing, we would tweak the truth. If pretending to respect someone we disliked would work in our favor, we played the part. We chose the easy way over the right way.

Integrity means the outside accurately reflects the inside; it's when our public image is the same as our private image. Having integrity means that when casual acquaintances say positive things about us, our spouse and children won't be saying, "Who are they talking about?"

It's been said that integrity is doing the right thing even when you're all alone and no one will find out what you did. J. C. Watts said, "There are too many people who think that the only thing that's right is to get by, and the only thing that's wrong is to get caught."[1] We don't want to be one of those people.

Integrity is the basis of trust. A life without integrity is like a house that's just been painted but the boards are filled with termites; it looks nice but lacks integrity. Over time the house begins to crumble.

Shaky relationships remind me of an old wooden stepladder I used to own. When I used it for painting or reaching, I always wondered when it was going to fall apart as it swayed and creaked with each step. When I was on it, I was thinking constantly about where I would jump if it started coming apart. Finally, I bought a new aluminum ladder. When I use it, I don't even think about it. I'm so confident that it won't fall apart that I trust it completely and am able to focus 100 percent on the task at hand.

That's what integrity does in relationships. Our experience with high-integrity people gives us so much confidence in that relationship that we don't question its strength.

The Impact of Integrity on Relationships

When we know we can trust someone, it becomes the base on which we can build a healthy connection with them. When we can't trust them, it influences everything that happens between us. No matter what they say or do, we question their motives and find ourselves evaluating their words, wondering if what they're saying can be trusted.

Without integrity, there is no foundation for a relationship to grow. In an earlier chapter, we talked about the need to base everything on truth instead of on our feelings and assumptions. With integrity, we not only need to know what is accurate and real around us, but we need to have truth inside of us. We need to *be* true.

People will only trust us if we prove ourselves trustworthy. We become trustworthy as people watch us over time and see our integrity. We can't just tell someone they can trust us; they have to observe it for themselves. If we're not being real, they might be impressed at first but will sense over time that we're just a movie set held up by scaffolding.

A wife tells her husband, "You never tell me you love me anymore." The husband replies, "I told you that when I married you. If it changes, I'll let you know." Maybe he does love her, and he might even say, "Yeah, I love you." But the words will be meaningless unless his actions demonstrate his care for her. Integrity means the words and actions consistently match.

We can't force anyone to have integrity. The only person we have control of is ourselves. Having integrity won't change others, but it does provide a foundation for what our relationships will look like. No matter how people respond to us, if we display integrity they'll recognize that we're operating from a solid core.

Someone said that if you have integrity, nothing else matters. If you don't have integrity, nothing else matters. It's the foundation for every healthy relationship.

Faking Integrity

Pretending to have integrity takes a lot of work. It's like pushing a cart through the grocery store and hitting a grape on the floor. The grape sticks to one of the wheels, and that wheel won't turn. We move the cart back and forth trying to dislodge it, but to no avail. Yes, we can keep shopping, but the experience turns into a negative one because we're fighting the grape the whole time.

Movie actors experience this when they're playing a part. They have to convince the audience that they really are someone else. But after the scene is over, they can't stay in that role forever. If they pretended to actually be that character in public, people would be amused but no one would believe them. So they play the part during the filming and are usually exhausted at the end because of the energy it took pretending to be something they are not.

Mark Twain said that if you always tell the truth, you don't have to have a good memory.[2] That's the way integrity is; if we actually have it, we won't wear ourselves out pretending that we do.

My father-in-law worked for a gas utility his entire career. One of his responsibilities was to teach new field workers how to weld steel pipe. They would practice until they felt they had welded a successful joint. My father-in-law would then put the welded pipe in a machine that twisted the metal until it broke. If it was a good weld, the metal would break first, not the weld. If the weld had integrity, it was stronger than the steel.

That's what integrity is like in our lives. It provides strength that doesn't break when we get twisted by the pressure of another person's choices. That doesn't mean we have to be tough and forceful with others; rather, we've developed the inner strength to stand firm when we're challenged by others.

Crazy people often use logic to make us crazy, and they're usually good at it. Under the pressure of emotion, it's easy to assume their logic is true. We let it mess with our heads, and we feel like we have to respond perfectly. But integrity is about us, not about them. Building integrity means we're strengthening the truth in our lives, building the security that stays strong no matter what the other person does.

If we're faking integrity, we might look like a good weld. But when the pressure comes, we'll break.

Protecting Our Integrity

Having integrity isn't like getting a college degree, where you graduate once and have the degree for the rest of your life. We have to constantly guard our integrity so we don't lose it. King Solomon said, "Guard your heart, for everything you do flows from it" (Prov. 4:23).

Wouldn't it be great if we could buy a new car and never have to wash it? Unfortunately, that car is constantly exposed to polluted air, bird droppings, tree sap, and dust. That's why we need to regularly apply a coat of wax to protect the finish. When we do, the dirt and droppings still land on the car but come off with a quick rinse. Without that protection, the pollutants gradually begin to eat into the paint and compromise the integrity of the finish.

We live in a society that bombards us with reasons to give up our integrity, tempting us to compromise what's right for what's convenient.

It's naïve to assume that our integrity is protected, that we're strong enough to handle the negative inputs around us (including the impact of crazy people). We need a good coat of wax and a regular rinse to keep our "paint" intact. Just as it's easier to keep the paint nice than to bring back the luster once it's gone, it's easier to maintain our integrity than to recover it once it's lost.

How can we protect our integrity?

Stay Close to the Healthy People in Our Lives

We become like the people we spend the most time with. Some people make us better and stronger when we're with them, and others drain us. Life dictates that we'll have to spend time with both types of people. But our integrity will grow if we consciously plan time with the people who build into our lives.

When our emotions are running on empty, we have nothing left to refill our own tank. We need to spend time with those whose emotional tanks are full and who are willing to share.

Be Conscious of Our Inputs

My dad once tried to bake a chocolate marble cake for my mom. The recipe said to "take two cups of batter and set it aside, add melted chocolate, and then swirl it back in." But my dad misread the word "batter" and added two cups of "butter." That's four sticks of the yellow stuff. When the cake came out, it was about a half inch thick and weighed about five pounds. Whatever goes into the cake determines how the final product turns out.

That's true of our character as well. Our integrity is a product of what we think. What we think will be determined by our inputs. The adage "Garbage in, garbage out" applies here.

For years, my wife and I have watched the news as a way to wind down before going to bed. Generally, I can go to sleep immediately. But I often wake up after about four hours and can't go back to sleep for a long time. I also frequently have uncomfortable dreams throughout the night and wake up feeling unsettled and not rested.

Recently, I've been thinking about what I see on the news at night. Most of it is negative, highlighting crime, economic problems, and corruption. The last inputs I have before going to bed have been negative. So I've switched to watching the early evening news and wrapping up any stimulating inputs about forty-five minutes before bedtime. I might read something that doesn't get my mind in high gear, or I simply sit in the dark on our patio for a while. I've discovered that my dreams have been much more positive, and I wake up feeling more refreshed. I might still wake up in the night, but I feel relaxed and can usually go back to sleep fairly quickly.

When I'm concerned about the actions or words of the crazy people in my life, I've learned the value of consciously replacing those thoughts with positive inputs: reading something uplifting, spending time in Scripture, walking through our local park, or connecting with the people who build positively into my life.

Be Intentional in Our Relationships with Crazy People

When we get "dumped on" by the crazy people in our lives, it's important to take time out to keep it from eating away at our integrity. We need to wash the bird droppings off the hood. People can only mess up our lives if we give them permission, so it's critical to do the regular maintenance to make sure we're operating from a solid foundation.

The Bottom Line on Integrity

Let's draw from the wisdom of others in developing and keeping our integrity:

> Live your life in such a way that you would not be ashamed to sell your parrot to the town gossip. (Will Rogers)

You can outdistance that which is running after you, but not what is running inside you. (Rwandan proverb)

Don't try to be better than others; try to be better than yourself. (Unknown)

Try to be the kind of person your dog already thinks you are. (Unknown)

16

Key #7—Go the Distance in Relationships

What's the value of commitment?

Hernando Cortez understood commitment. According to legend, it was the early 1500s and the Spanish conquistador was committed to conquering the Aztec empire. The problem was that the Aztec empire had almost six million people. Cortez had arrived with only 508 soldiers, 100 sailors, and 16 horses. He was outnumbered roughly 10,000 to 1—not the best odds for victory.

He knew that fear could wipe out his tiny army's commitment and they would be tempted to retreat. So he burned the boats in which they had arrived, making retreat impossible. The only options left were to either win or die.

But while burning the boats was designed to build the commitment of his soldiers, it had an even greater impact on the huge, highly trained Aztec army. They recognized that these Spanish soldiers would be fighting for their lives with no possibility of turning back. Since their Aztec empire was so large, it was easy for them to retreat when things got tough.

Which is exactly what happened. Two years later, the little Spanish army had conquered the Aztec nation. What they lacked in size, training, and military equipment, they made up for with total commitment.

Burning Your Boats

People who are known for having strong commitment have an edge in relationships. It gives them a foundation on which to manage their connections, even (especially) with the crazy people in their lives.

Why? Because commitment isn't the norm it used to be. Years ago, it was usually assumed that if someone promised something, they would find a way to carry it out, even when things got tough. Today, convenience has become the norm. We'll hang in there until it becomes uncomfortable, then we'll take the easy way out. Trust is at an all-time low in corporations, churches, and relationships. Since we've trusted others to fulfill their commitments so many times and been disappointed when they don't, we have trouble believing their promises in the future.

In traditional wedding vows, the bride and groom make their promises "before God and these witnesses." That sounds like commitment. It really says, "With God and all these people as my witness, I'll fulfill my promises to you. I won't let you down." We promise to be true to the other person "in sickness and in health, for richer or for poorer, for better or for worse." But in reality, the vows turn out to be "in health . . . for richer . . . for better." When "sickness," "poorer," or "worse" show up, somebody in the relationship disappears.

Over half of marriages end in divorce when those promises aren't kept. A 2011 study revealed that more Americans are choosing not to marry than actually tie the knot. One reason cited was that they'd rather not make commitments, knowing that they will probably be broken anyway.[1]

What would happen if we found a way to "burn our boats" in relationships? What if we developed a level of commitment where people absolutely believed that we wouldn't run when things got uncomfortable?

It would do something for us because retreat wouldn't be an option. It would do something for the other person because they could count on us.

What If I Make the Wrong Choice?

My son Tim and I were at a restaurant that has a twenty-page menu. It's a great restaurant, but it takes me forever to decide on a meal because there are so many choices. This particular night, Tim picked up the menu, glanced at the first page for about ten seconds, and put it back on the table.

"What's wrong?" I asked.

"Nothing. I've already decided what I want."

"But you've only looked at one page," I countered.

"Right. In a restaurant like this, I've learned to just read through the menu from the beginning until I find something that looks good, and that's what I get. The next time we come here, I'll start from that place in the menu and move forward and do it again."

I thought about that for a while and realized what a wise choice that was. When we have too many choices, we get paralyzed because we're afraid we'll make a mistake. "What if I order something and then see something I like better? Will I regret my first choice?" Tim has overcome that dilemma by making his decision then putting the menu down so he doesn't have to compare.

That happens in many areas of life. People are afraid to make a decision about a purchase, a job, a house, or a spouse because they're worried they'll make the commitment and then find something "better." We assume that it's better to skip the commitment so we'll have the freedom to look around in the future.

For example, it's hard to make a marriage work with that mind-set. A couple commits to each other, but they wonder if they've made a mistake when things get tough. If retreat is an option, they'll be much more inclined to leave the relationship. But if they have burned their boats, there is a greater incentive to work through the challenges and make the relationship work.

Trying to make the perfect decision can paralyze us. In our family, we've often said, "You might not be able to make the right decision. But once you make the decision, make it right." It means putting the menu down after you place your order.

The Payoff of Persistence

I've never washed or waxed a rental car. I don't purposely abuse them, and I'm careful not to get them scratched or dented. But since it's not my car and I only have it for one day (and I'm paying a lot of money for it), I don't treat it quite the same as my own car. Sometimes I'll drive it a little harder than normal or take it over rough roads I might otherwise avoid. In my own car, hitting a pothole concerns me because I might have messed up the alignment, creating excessive tire wear and other problems down the line. In a rental car, I don't give it a second thought since I won't have the car after one day. Deep inside I'm thinking, "It's not my problem" and "I'm paying them to worry about this." (OK, maybe I was having a bad day . . .)

I also know that someone else will be driving that car tomorrow, and they have their own driving habits and issues. If the car is rented every day, it has 365 drivers each year who aren't committed to the car's long-term care. They treat the car differently because they're not committed for the long haul. They don't care if it's washed, waxed, or maintained. They just want it to work for them all day long, and then they turn it in when they don't need it anymore.

Making a commitment shows ownership in a relationship. If we operate from a filter that says we're committed 24/7, 365 days a year, we don't treat the relationship as a rental. We wash it, wax it, and take the steps to maintain it.

"A car is one thing," you say. "I can pick my car, but I don't pick the crazy people who are part of my life—my co-workers, my neighbors, and my in-laws and out-laws. I might have picked the situation, but they came as part of the package. They're there, and I can't just get rid of them."

It's true. In those long-term crazy relationships, we might feel like we're at the mercy of others. If we focus on the fact that they are in our lives by default, we'll never be free from the emotional strain of those ties. It's only when we *accept* and *adapt* that we have a real chance for a healthy outlook.

Accepting means that we don't fight the inevitable. We come to terms with the reality of their presence in our lives. *Adapting* means that since we can't change that reality, we make it the basis for how we respond. We change ourselves.

Sometimes it might be appropriate to separate ourselves from crazy people, such as when our lives or the lives of those we care about are in danger. But when withdrawing is our default solution, we never get to experience the positive things that come from working on a relationship over a long period of time.

Keeping Peace or Making Peace?

Nate grew up in a family that avoided conflict. It became a pattern in his adult life and he always saw himself as a peacemaker. He didn't run away from tough relationships, so he felt that showed his commitment. But he always avoided the tough issues between family members, so his relationships were comfortable—on the surface.

Then he married Vicki, whose family practiced conflict as a recreational activity. Over fifteen years of marriage and with three growing sons, Nate stayed committed through the tough times. But when they occurred, he found himself trying to keep everyone happy instead of working through the issues. He was the peacemaker.

Nate wanted to be a better husband and dad, so he spent some time with a counselor to learn more about himself and gain tools for growing. When he described his tendency to hold the role of a peacemaker, the counselor said, "Actually, you're not a peacemaker. You're a peacekeeper. A peacekeeper tries to *keep* things the way they are. A peacemaker is willing to face the issues and do the hard work to *make* peace."

Nate and Vicki are at a healthy place in their marriage and are still growing. Nate is still wired to keep the peace but has learned the value of making peace. He doesn't like tough conversations but chooses to engage in them when necessary. But neither of them would be where they are without commitment. If they had bailed out during the many tough times, they wouldn't be the people they are today.

Unfortunately, it doesn't surprise us that people disappear when things get tough. That's why it has such an impact on a relationship when we're convinced the other person is in it for the long haul, even if we're being a jerk. Growth happens in committed relationships that wouldn't happen in any other way.

Football coach Vince Lombardi once said, "Once a man has made a commitment to a way of life, he puts the greatest strength in the world behind him. It's something we call heart power. Once a man has made this commitment, nothing will stop him short of success."[2]

Simply stated, burning our boats is the best way to build healthy relationships and handle the crazy ones.

Growing Commitment

So, how do we learn commitment when we've been conditioned against it?

Think about the people who have shown their commitment to you. Can you think of someone in your life whom you tend to take for granted because they're so consistently dedicated to you? What difference has that commitment made in your relationship? What is different about that relationship than other ones, because you're convinced they're not going away?

The difference usually involves some form of unconditional love. They're not always trying to fix us but accept us just the way we are. By providing that foundation, they can challenge us honestly to grow. Even if we don't grow, they're still there for us.

Sheila took some pretty wild turns in her teenage years. Her journey strayed far from her parents' values (and her own). But years later the healing began. She told her parents, "No matter how far I strayed and how bad my choices were, the one thing that kept bringing me back was knowing that you still loved me, no matter what. You expressed it. You didn't like what I was doing, and I hurt you deeply. I knew you were disappointed and angry at times, but I never doubted your love."

Solomon said, "It is better not to make a vow than to make one and not fulfill it" (Eccles. 5:5). Commitment is when you promise something and keep your promise. That should be a characteristic of our lives, and it's a characteristic of those who have the inner strength to handle crazy people effectively.

Think about the things you've promised. How are you doing on your commitment to those promises? It doesn't matter if the person you're married to isn't perfect, if your kids are driving you nuts, or if your boss has lost his mind. This isn't about them; it's about *you*.

Commitment is your greatest resource for impacting the people around you, whether they're crazy or not.

Part 4

Changing Your Environment

17

Prioritize Your Relationships

Have you ever noticed that the older we get, the busier we become? Each year that passes brings new opportunities, new challenges, and new relationships. It's not like hundreds of people suddenly come into our lives. But each new commitment or relationship adds to the ones we already have until we feel inundated:

- Someone recommends a book that's exactly what we were looking for.
- We hear about a "must visit" restaurant that's opened.
- An old friend connects with us through social media.
- New opportunities at church promise personal growth and outreach.
- We begin a new relationship that we want to nurture.
- A promotion at work provides a bump in pay but greater responsibility.
- We're taking classes toward a degree and have to do extensive homework.

- Growing kids means growing demands on our time, energy, and sanity.

Notice the common thread: these are all *good* things. It's not like we're subscribing to the vice-of-the-month club. These are all things we believe can make our life richer, so we want to add them all.

The problem is that we add new activities without getting rid of any old ones. We're not replacing good commitments with better ones; we're simply making a longer list. When we have trouble giving the proper level of attention to each one, we feel guilty.

Marco described his dilemma several weeks ago while attending one of my seminars. He's a seasoned musician, composer, and recording artist, having spent the past fifteen years on concert stages around the world. Now he wants to shift gears and invest in young musicians, using his own experience to mentor them on their career paths.

"I've made a lot of relationships around the world over those years," he said, "and I don't want to give them up. But if I move in this new direction, it's going to take a lot of time and energy. I'll be developing new relationships as this new focus takes off. So how do I build new quality relationships while still maintaining the old ones?"

That's a real dilemma. Most of us face some version of that every day. We add new but we don't want to subtract old. Soon our closets, garages, file cabinets, and even our minds become stuffed to the point that we feel out of control.

To find a good solution, we have to accept one absolute, irrefutable, undeniable fact:

Time is limited. We only have twenty-four hours in a day.

Opportunity Cost

As long as we believe we can do everything and have it all, we'll never solve the problem of being overcommitted. We'll take time management seminars and read self-help books to find ways to cram more into our lives. Those will actually help for a while, but it's like rearranging the deck chairs on the *Titanic*. It may look better, but it won't keep the ship from going down.

We might think of a person we know who gets more done than us. It's easy to think, "Well, they must have more time than I do." But they have twenty-four hours, just like we have twenty-four hours. Somehow, they're more productive than we are.

However, there's a greater problem. It doesn't matter if we're doing *more* things if we're not doing the *right* things.

In economics, the concept is called "opportunity cost." It means that whatever you say yes to, you're automatically saying no to everything else at that time. If you spend an hour in a meeting, you're not exercising, cleaning, or reading during that time. If you're talking to a friend on the phone, you're giving up the opportunity to wash your car. If you take the kids to Disneyland, you're not mowing the lawn.

Those are all good things, but we can only do one thing at a time. Since time is limited, we can't do everything. The only way to survive is to prioritize our choices, deciding which ones would be the best use of our time.

Suppose your house caught on fire and you knew it would be engulfed in flames within minutes. What would you take with you as you ran out the door? Almost everyone gives the same answer: the things that have the most value. The list usually consists of family members, pets, photo albums, and other irreplaceable items. No one rushes back into a burning house to get their favorite mug.

Relationship Cost

The more value something has to us, the more careful we are. That's why we try not to drop our laptop or balance a glass of lemonade on the keyboard.

That principle applies to our relationships as well. We might have a lot of relationships we enjoy, and we value the uniqueness of each connection. But we're limited in the amount of time and energy we have available. When we spend time with one person, we're giving up the opportunity to spend time with someone else. Though it might sound heartless, we need to prioritize our relationships, spending appropriate amounts of time with different people based on their value in our lives.

My wife Diane is more important to me than anyone on the planet. I have a lifelong commitment to her, which means I need to invest most heavily in that relationship. I also have a career and have discovered that certain people tend to think that I should show up. My job is a valuable part of my life and requires a solid chunk of time and commitment. But that takes time away from Diane.

Sometimes I travel, so I'm gone for several days at a time. When that happens, I don't get to spend time with my wife. When I return home, there are many people I could catch up with. But even though those are good relationships, I've learned the value of investing in Diane first. I might change jobs or locations or other situations, but I'm not planning on changing wives.

What Does That Have to Do with Crazy People?

Crazy people tend to suck up more of our energy than they deserve. They bring drama into our lives, which moves us away from our set point, and we instinctively try to solve the problem so we find our balance again. Their presence can take large amounts of our time and energy, which means there's little left for other people.

All relationships are not created equal. The only hope we have for finding balance is to prioritize our relationships, giving appropriate time to people based on their value in our lives. The more valuable they are to us, the more of our focus they should receive. The less connected we are to them, the less focus we give them.

Once we've made that distinction, we can keep certain crazy people from hijacking our emotions. If our spouse or another family member is that crazy person, they deserve more of our emotional energy than a cranky neighbor or a co-worker who whistles. But when people who are an occasional blip on our radar screen become noisy, it seems harder for us to ignore.

I run into this occasionally during seminars. With fifty people in a room, I might have forty-nine who are tracking with me and one who just isn't getting it. That one might be challenging what I'm saying simply because they want to disagree, not because they honestly have questions. It's tempting to try to "rescue" them and bring them back on board. But if I spend time during the class trying to fix them, I'll lose the rest of the class. I can't rob the other participants in order to go after that one; I need to take time during a break to work with that individual privately.

How Leaders Do It

Jesus is a great example of someone who knew how to prioritize relationships. We know he loved everyone and was quick to meet the needs of people. But he spent more time with the people he was closest to and less time with everyone else. We see him speaking to thousands of people at a time, giving them the words they needed to hear. But he invested heavily in his twelve disciples, giving them his time and energy.

Among the twelve, Jesus had three individuals into whom he poured his life. He invested the greatest time and energy in this small group, and they were the ones who went on to change the world.

Ask the head of any large nonprofit, and they'll tell you the challenge they feel in leading an organization that is too large for them to connect with each person individually. They'll speak to volunteers at conferences and be as available as possible. But they know time is limited; so they work with a group of leaders in the organization and equip them to meet the needs of the volunteers. Even among those leaders, they will have several key individuals they connect with on a deeper level, who in turn carry their passion into the organization.

My wife and I mentored in a class for young married couples at our church for eleven years. We started with them when our kids left home and we became empty nesters because we had emotional energy to invest in other people. We got to walk with them through the early stages of their marriages and share in the joys and challenges of their growing families. Over time they became our friends.

But over a decade later, our priorities began to shift. Changes in our jobs, the birth of grandchildren, and new time pressures began filtering to the top of our list of priorities. It was a tough decision to leave the class because we cared for them so deeply. We knew that we had only a certain amount of time and energy to work with, and we made the shift.

Goethe wrote, "Things which matter most must never be at the mercy of things which matter least."[1] That's true in every area of life—including our relationships.

Structure for Sanity

Prioritizing our relationships won't solve every problem that comes up. What it will do is provide the structure on which to build, making sure that each person in our life receives the appropriate amount of focus:

- The closer we are to someone, the more focus they deserve.
- The further we are from someone, the less focus they deserve.

Yesterday I pulled up to a crowded intersection. As I came to a stop, I heard yelling nearby. Several lanes over, someone had gotten out of his car at the red light, stomped back to the car behind him, and was totally out of control with anger. I couldn't see who was in the other car, whether they were responding or not, or what their reaction was. The angry man was jumping up and down, pointing, and swearing at the top of his lungs. After a few minutes the signal changed, and he stormed back to his car and peeled out across the street.

I don't know if he knew the other driver or not. They might have been related, but I'm guessing it was a stranger who did something to upset him. Typically, someone with that level of anger doesn't just get it out of their system and feel better. They would probably drive like a maniac for the next few miles, endangering the lives of other drivers nearby. Then they would go home and rant to family members about how upset they were.

That would be an inappropriate level of focus for a complete stranger. But that's what happens too often when we allow crazy people to take us where we don't want to go. We give them more time and emotional energy than they deserve. When that happens, it robs the people who are most important to us of the time and emotional energy that *they* deserve. At the same time, we cheat ourselves by the drain it places on our own energy.

So, how do we start the process of reallocating our time?

Think of it like our personal finances. Money has no value by itself; it's just paper and ink. Money gains value when we decide what we're going to do with it. If we take it to a restaurant, it has the value of food. If we take it to a theater, it has the value of entertainment.

We've heard the saying "Time is money." In a lot of ways, that's true. Just like money, an hour has no value by itself; it's just a unit of time. It gains value when we decide what we're going to do with it. If I spend an hour with my kids, I've given it the value of family. If I spend an hour at work, it has the value of employment.

There is one primary difference, though, between time and money. We can choose not to spend our money; we can save it, set it aside, or invest it. But we can't do that with time. We're going to spend every minute we have. Whatever we choose to spend it on, that's the value it has for us. That also means we're not spending it on anyone or anything else. Once it's spent, it's gone.

That's opportunity cost. We will spend every hour that we have. If we don't determine where we're going to spend it, then someone else will decide for us.

Who deserves the best of your time today?

18

No Guarantees

Alison goes to the gym four times a week. She joined a spin class and a yoga class. She doesn't eat red meat, grows her own vegetables, and drinks purified water. She takes supplements and wears sunscreen.

Patrick eats bacon four times a week. He watches weight-loss reality shows on television while eating chips. His weight lifting program consists of standing up. He eats mayonnaise from the jar with his fingers. He has installed a soda tap in his garage.

So, who's going to live the longest?

Alison has taken every precaution to protect her health, but she could get hit by a texting driver while walking through a parking lot. Patrick could defy the odds and live to be a hundred.

Is it fair? No. There are no guarantees in life. We plan for the worst but hope for the best. Neither Alison nor Patrick can control every aspect of their lives. Normally, our choices determine our outcomes; but the outcomes are not guaranteed. The only things we have control over are the choices, not the results.

How Long Before My Crazy People Change?

Earlier in this book, we established that we can't change others. We can only change ourselves. If we think that by hanging in there long enough they'll come around, we'll probably be disappointed. The only way we can avoid being a victim is to make the right choices because those choices are right, not because they might convince someone to change.

It's hard to stay motivated when our crazy person doesn't change. Our willpower runs out, our tank runs dry, and we think, "When will things get better?"

There are no guarantees. It might not get better. They might never change. The only way we can be drama-free in our relationships is to focus on us, not them. We're the ones who can change.

Making healthy choices in our relationships isn't a one-time decision that lasts forever. To stay motivated, we have to keep making those choices day by day, over and over. Zig Ziglar used to say, "People often say that motivation doesn't last. Well, neither does bathing—that's why we recommend it daily."[1]

Relationships Don't Come with Guarantees

Humor columnist Erma Bombeck once said, "Marriage has no guarantees. If that's what you're looking for, go live with a car battery."[2]

A guarantee is a promise that something will perform as expected. We buy a new car or appliance and we expect it to do what the brochure promised. If that doesn't happen, the manufacturer will either fix it or replace it. Most people won't make a major purchase without that type of guarantee.

Wouldn't it be great if relationships came with guarantees? Any time someone in our lives got crazy, we could call up the store and trade them in for a better model. "I'm sorry," we would say, "this one isn't working. I think we have a lemon. When can I bring him back?"

Life doesn't work that way, however. Like a used car, our relationships come "as is." When something goes wrong, we can try to fix it or work around it. But no matter what we do, the other person might stay broken (which implies that we're *not* broken). In our society it's common for people to quickly discard relationships when they don't live up to expectations, as evidenced by the high divorce rate. But if we're committed for the long haul, we have to distinguish between the things we can change and the things we can't change.

What can we *not* change? Other people. What *can* we change? Ourselves. What do we do when the other person doesn't change? *Accept* (the reality of the situation) and *adapt* (change the way we think and respond).

The Bible is filled with passages that describe the need to take responsibility for ourselves rather than others. Look at some examples from just one chapter, Romans 14:

> "Who are you to judge someone else's servant? To their own master, servants stand or fall." (verse 4)
>
> "You, then, why do you judge your brother or sister? Or why do you treat them with contempt?" (verse 10)
>
> "Each of us will give an account of ourselves to God." (verse 12)
>
> "Let us stop passing judgment on one another." (verse 13)

The principle is simple: We are only responsible for our own choices and actions. We're not responsible for the choices of others.

So, What's My Job?

If you've had teenagers, you've probably experienced the dilemma. It's our responsibility to guide our kids as they grow into adulthood, and we provide boundaries to steer them in the right direction. The purpose is to help them become responsible adults, being able to function independently and make wise decisions. The older they get, the more the responsibility for those choices transfers from us to them.

Yesterday I went to a park near our house. As I sat by the lake, I watched a family of ducks swimming near the shoreline. The parents swam with one of their ducklings while the second duckling paddled off by itself in a different direction. Soon, several other ducks surrounded the duckling in what appeared to be a threatening way. The duckling began to panic.

The mother left her family and moved toward the group until the other ducks moved away. She then guided her duckling gently back to her family.

Once they were back together, she pecked the little duck so hard he completely submerged in the water. As soon as he came back up, she did it again. He barely broke the surface before it happened a third time.

After that, he stayed with his family. Don't mess with mama duck . . .

Why did she do that? I can't peek inside duck brains, but I'm guessing she was teaching her duckling the importance of boundaries. Within a few months, that duckling will grow up and be on its own. By then it will either know about boundaries or it won't. Either way, the mother duck won't be responsible for her duckling's choices any more.

Our kids are both adults. We're involved in their lives, and we're there for support (and guidance if they ask). But we're not responsible for their choices and have to accept the fact that over time they will probably make decisions we would consider crazy. We did the same with our parents, and they thought we were crazy.

There's a great story in the biblical book of Ezekiel that stars a grandfather, his son, and his grandson (see Ezek. 18:5–20). The grandfather lived an honorable life, doing everything right. His son did exactly the opposite, doing everything wrong. The grandson reversed the pattern again and did everything right. Who's responsible for whom?

The passage states that each person is responsible for their own behavior. "The child will not share the guilt of the parent, nor will the parent share the guilt of the child. The righteousness of the righteous will be credited to them, and the wickedness of the wicked will be charged against them" (Ezek. 18:20).

That holds true with everyone in our lives. We're responsible for us; they're responsible for them. Knowing that is the foundation for dealing with the crazy people in our lives. We can't guarantee that we can fix them, but we can focus on how we respond to them. Sometimes that means confronting them, setting up boundaries, or taking steps to protect ourselves and our families emotionally and physically. Sometimes it will mean more contact, sometimes less.

That brings us back to an earlier concept in this book: *expectation* versus *expectancy*. When we have *expectations* that another person will change, we're setting ourselves up for disappointment. We expect that if we do the right things, they will eventually change. But that's unrealistic, since it can't be guaranteed.

It's healthier to live in *expectancy*. That means we do everything in our power to change the situation, influence the other person, and hope for the best, accepting the fact that things might stay the way they are. Expectancy lives in reality but watches every relationship with anticipation of what could happen in the future.

My wife and I have a couple whom we've been close to for years. They've really struggled in their marriage, and we've invested a lot of time, energy, and resources coming alongside and loving them. We haven't had an agenda except to walk through the journey with them and be there for them. They have their ups and downs. Often they'll seem to be making progress; then a few weeks later they're struggling again, and we wonder if they'll be able to make it.

If we stayed close to them with the expectation of changing them, we'd be living by an inappropriate standard. The reason we stay involved with them is because we love them. We'll love them if they make it, and we'll love them if they don't. Sure, we'll be disappointed, but we'll still love them.

That's expectancy: realizing that with relationships there are no guarantees, but always anticipating the possibilities.

When dealing with crazy people, staying on our side of the relationship is the only way to keep from becoming a victim of their choices. When we work on ourselves and relate with integrity, we find the strength that allows us to make wise, healthy choices.

Who knows? They might change. If they don't, we've changed. Changing ourselves changes everything.

19

When to Leave

At forty, Jim has spent his entire career in the banking industry. He knows his way around banking like the back of his hand and could talk about finances in his sleep (and probably does). He's competent in his skills and confident in his abilities.

Over the years, Jim has worked at several different banking institutions. Good situations, bad situations—he's seen it all. But his last job stretched him to the limit. In his position as director of operations, he had responsibility for a large part of the organization. The bank was struggling, and Jim knew his input could move it back onto solid ground.

The problem was his boss. Usually, bosses are supposed to remove barriers for their employees, freeing them up to use their unique strengths to excel in their work. But this manager *was* the barrier. He wouldn't listen to Jim's ideas and micromanaged every detail of his position. Jim began to feel devalued and became discouraged and depressed about his situation.

Jim knew he couldn't continue this way long-term. Sure, he could have stormed into his boss's office and yelled, "I can't take it anymore.

You're crazy! I quit." But he knew that would be a reactive response and he would regret the consequences of that choice. Instead, he went through the healthy, three-step process discussed earlier in this book.

First, he tried to change the situation. He used logic, influence, and careful confrontation to change the dynamics of the relationship. He asked businesspeople he respected how they would handle things. He focused on supporting and affirming his superiors. But over time, nothing changed.

Second, he worked on his attitude. Convinced that the situation wouldn't change, Jim realized he could be a victim or a victor. It was easy to be a victim, letting his emotions be controlled by the environment he was in. That's where he began, feeling hopeless and mentally disengaging from his work. But input from caring friends was the catalyst for change. Instead of being a victim, he realized that for now, this was his job. He decided to focus on being dedicated, learning whatever he could from the bad situation while he was still there. He reengaged with his company, giving it his best effort in spite of the people around him. "The turning point," he said, "was when I remembered that I was really working for God, not for these people."

During that time, Jim took the third step: change his environment. He knew it wouldn't be healthy to stay in that situation long-term, so he started looking for a new opportunity. In a tight economy, it seemed like an uphill climb. But with consistent steps, he explored different opportunities while giving 100 percent in his current position. Several months later, he found a new position in a new industry.

The result was the same: he changed jobs. But it wasn't a knee-jerk reaction. He followed a three-step process to ensure the best outcome:

1. Change the situation
2. Change your attitude
3. Change your environment

Jim grew through the process and was able to have a healthy attitude when he left his previous employer.

Our situation may involve different people, but the scenario is the same. Whether it's an unreasonable boss, interfering parents, a demanding spouse, undisciplined kids, nosy neighbors, insensitive friends, or crazy siblings, someone else's choices are creating havoc in our lives.

Sometimes we feel hopeless. We're trapped in a job or a relationship and don't see any way out:

- "I'm a single parent, and I can't quit my job."
- "My spouse is abusive, but I don't have anywhere to go."
- "My sister is driving me crazy, but you can't divorce your sister."
- "My parents stick their nose into everything I do, but I can't disrespect them."
- "If I confront them or end the relationship, they'll explode—and I don't think I'm ready for that."

These situations all involve people we care about. In fact, that's why they're driving us crazy. Someone we work with could show the same behaviors and we would think it was entertaining. But when it's someone we care about and we feel stuck with them, the situation seems hopeless.

When the tension builds, we wonder how much longer we can put up with it. Everything inside us wants to run away and escape the situation.

So, is leaving a bad thing?

In most cases, it's bad if it's a reactive response. But if it's the last resort of a carefully thought-out process, it could be the healthiest solution.

Should I Leave or Stay?

Since every situation is different, we can't have a one-size-fits-all checklist. That would be handy, but there are as many solutions as there are situations. Generally, all of the solutions fit into one of three actions:

1. Stay in a bad situation
2. Leave a bad situation
3. Stay in a bad situation with a strategy for working on it

Stay in a Bad Situation

Staying in a bad situation *with no plan for changing the situation or our response* is almost always a bad idea. Ignoring the problems we face won't make them go away. We hope things will get better and that our crazy person will change.

Yes, it's possible—but so is winning the lottery. We know the chances of winning big are almost nonexistent, but we keep buying tickets "just in case." As the old adage says, "If you continue to do what you've always done, you'll continue to get what you've always gotten." If you want anything to be different, you have to do things differently.

Why do people stay in bad situations? There could be a number of reasons:

- They're afraid of what the crazy person will do if they quit the job or end the relationship.
- They're afraid of what will happen to them if they pull out.
- They're afraid of what other people will say.
- They're afraid of the unknown.
- They've always been a victim, so they don't know any other way of living.
- They listen to advice from well-meaning friends who are trying to fix them.
- They're afraid of conflict.
- They're trying to protect the crazy person.

Most of those reasons have to do with *fear*. That might seem unreasonable, but people have an emotional set point within any situation where the pain is more comfortable than the prospect of the unknown.

That's why people often stay in jobs with an abusive boss: it's all they know, whereas taking positive steps is risky.

One of the most dangerous reasons to stay in a bad situation is trying to protect the crazy person. We make excuses for their behavior because we don't want people to think badly of them or because they embarrass us. The problem is that when we protect them, we shield them from the negative consequences of their behavior. If they don't have consequences, they never have an incentive to change. They might apologize and promise things will be different, but promises have to be backed up with performance. Blind loyalty on our part can actually keep healing from happening.

Staying in a bad situation without any plan for change is like constantly putting air in a leaky tire without patching the hole.

Leave a Bad Situation

Leaving should be a calculated choice, making it the last resort after all other options have been exhausted. It might involve quitting a job, changing churches, or moving from a toxic friendship. Leaving too quickly and impulsively rids us of the uncomfortable situation but doesn't resolve the issues that led to the problem in the first place.

Every relationship problem involves interaction between two or more people. The crazy person may be primarily at fault, but we need to consider our contribution as well—how we respond, what we say, the choices we make. If we aren't being realistic by recognizing the reality of our part in the problem, we'll carry those same responses and attitudes into the next situation.

"OK," you say, "I've tried everything possible to change the situation, and it won't budge. They're still crazy. I've worked on my attitude and response, but I'm running out of ammunition. At what point should I consider a change?"

Again, there are no absolutes. But here are the questions to ask yourself:

169

- Am I unable to keep from being a victim?
- Do I see myself as less of a person because of the other person's choices?
- Am I (or the people I'm responsible for) in danger?
- What, exactly, will I be giving up if I leave?
- What, exactly, will it cost me to stay?
- If I leave, what steps can I take to genuinely resolve these questions?

If you answered yes to any of the first three questions, that doesn't necessarily mean you should make a change. But when added to your answers to the last three questions, it provides the foundation for making a careful decision.

Stay in the Situation, but with a Plan

There's a big difference between staying in a bad situation with no plan and staying with a carefully crafted blueprint. The first is wishful thinking; the second provides genuine hope.

If we make the choice to stay, it shouldn't be because we feel obligated to "hang in there." It should be because we've determined that there is (a) sufficient value in the relationship to make it worth the effort, and (b) sufficient evidence that the other person is willing to participate in the change. If they're not willing to work on it, they won't see any consequences, which means there will be no change. We don't want to impulsively quit a dysfunctional job without something else lined up, but we become victims if we stay without a course of action for improving the situation.

It takes effort to make a blueprint for relationships. It's not quite as hard with casual, irritating relationships. With a spouse or family member, getting help from a professional counselor could be a valuable resource for charting a new course. In any case, the plan needs to design ways of coping with our anger and hurt when it happens, as well as strategies for dealing with painful issues as they arise. We also need a clear delineation of physical and emotional boundaries for the other person. "Good fences make good neighbors," as Robert Frost said. If we're going to stay, we need a plan.

Staying Power

If we decide to stay in a situation, committing energy to make it work, here are suggestions to survive and thrive:

- Think through your options. Be sure that the plan is in place before making the decision.
- Decide what your nonnegotiables are if you stay—the boundaries that will keep the plan on task.
- Find a way to be yourself in the relationship. Pretending that you're OK can drain your energy over time and keep the relationship from growing.
- Base everything on truth. Be willing to set aside your fears, prejudices, and inaccurate lenses to see things the way they really are. Look at the facts behind the feelings.
- Look at the time you remain in the relationship as a test period where you both work on how you relate to each other. That provides a chance to evaluate evidence of growth or decay. If things fail to progress, go back to the decision-making process about staying or leaving.
- It's never healthy to be a martyr. Don't base your identity on the fact that you're hanging in there in a debilitating relationship.
- Take ownership of your decision. Recognize that there will be no perfect choice, because every decision has good and bad outcomes. Instead of trying to make exactly the right choice, make a healthy choice and then make it right.
- Let the other person take ownership of their side of the relationship. We need to take care of ourselves and let them take care of

themselves. Instead of rescuing them, we need to let them make their choices and reap the consequences of those choices.

Committing to a Decision

Write down the names of three people you have the most challenging relationship with and why. Rank them based on their level of challenge. Take the top one and ask: What would be the worst thing that would happen if I *left* this relationship? What would be the best thing? What would be the worst thing that would happen if I *stayed* in this relationship? What would be the best thing?

Then show the list to a trusted, objective friend to evaluate if you're seeing clearly or if your own lens is distorted.

There are no easy answers, but looking at our relationships with eyes wide open, we can evaluate and make decisions with wisdom.

Staying in a toxic relationship without a plan is a dangerous choice. Wavering in our decision making isn't healthy either. We might choose to leave, or we might choose to stay. Staying in the middle is a recipe for disaster.

Part 5

Putting It into Practice

20

Giving Up on Getting Straight A's

Kim has a clean house. OK, not just clean. Immaculate. When she gets up in the morning, she immediately makes the bed. She makes breakfast but wouldn't think of going to work before washing the dishes and putting everything away. She vacuums every other day, and more often if people might be dropping by. The car is always washed and the plants are trimmed. Kim doesn't have a lot of free time and often feels overwhelmed by how much there is to do. If a burglar broke in during the day, he would think he was in a model home.

Is it bad to have a clean house? That depends on the motive. Kim might really enjoy cleaning and the satisfaction that comes from living in an organized environment. But if she does it to build an image of perfection, it's unhealthy. She never gets to enjoy the results because she's so concerned about getting it just right.

Kim's perfectionism carries over to work as well. She often turns in projects at the last minute because she keeps revising them. She wouldn't think of submitting an assignment that's less than perfect, because someone might not think well of her. She sets unusually high standards for her own performance and her career path, believing that it's a demonstration of personal excellence. Her co-workers respect her drive and initiative, but she wonders why none of them have become close friends with her.

There's a fine line between *excellence* and *perfection*. While we can attain excellence, we'll never achieve perfection—and we'll wear ourselves out trying.

Why Do We Strive for Perfection?

Perfectionism might seem like a strange topic to include when we're talking about crazy people. But when we're involved with those people, it's one of the most common defenses used for survival.

Here's how it works:

We don't want people to think badly of us. It pulls us away from our set point, and everything inside us wants to get back to our comfort zone. We think, "If there's nothing to criticize about me, these crazy people will appreciate me." The closer we are to perfect, the less they'll have to critique.

Sounds logical, right? It seems like that should produce less stress because we aren't being evaluated or harassed. But for those who have experienced it, the stress level actually rises. No one can achieve perfection, and it can be exhausting trying to maintain that image over a long period of time. It takes an incredible amount of energy to micromanage every detail of our lives.

When we base our personal value on the opinions of other people, we crave their approval. We think that if people see imperfections in us, they won't like us. So being perfect becomes a way of avoiding that disapproval.

In *Why Am I Afraid to Tell You Who I Am?* John Powell makes this revealing statement: "I'm afraid to tell you who I am, because if I tell you who I am, you might not like who I am . . . and that's all I've got."[1] When we feel the need to appear perfect, we set ourselves up to be at the mercy of others' opinions. Our self-worth is based on what other people think of us, so we try to control their perceptions.

I did that when I was in high school and college. I didn't feel great about myself, so I tried to find ways to make people look up to me through the things I chose to do. My first job was working in the morgue at the county hospital in Phoenix (an incredibly cool job when you're a teenage boy). From there I worked in a music store, learned offset printing and worked in a print shop, got a job doing the afternoon on-air shift at a local radio station, and learned wedding photography with a studio in town. In other words, I picked the jobs that no one else was doing, hoping that others would be impressed with the unusual things I did.

It worked. They were impressed, and I received a lot of attention for what I was doing. But it didn't help my self-worth. I assumed that they were impressed with my actions, not with who I really was on the inside. I figured that if they really knew what I was like, they wouldn't be impressed at all. So I worked hard to maintain the image but felt worse and worse about myself when I was alone.

It took years to find my value in myself instead of in living for the attention and approval of others.

Parents often want the approval of others, so they make sure their kids are always on their best behavior in public. They don't want bad behavior reflecting on their parenting skills. Unfortunately, it's unhealthy for the kids and projects a false image of perfection.

Perfectionists usually grow up being valued for performance rather than character. They never experience unconditional love, so they equate acceptance with performance. They learn to believe that other people only see worth in them because of what they accomplish and how they do it. As adults, they view themselves in the same way, with their self-worth being a product of other people's opinions. They don't want to be criticized, so they try to become perfect.

The Dark Side of Perfectionism

It's natural to assume that perfectionism would be a pathway to success in life. After all, the better we perform, the more successful we'll be. Makes sense, right?

177

But it actually gets in the way of success. Since we never achieve perfection, we never feel satisfied about our performance. So we always feel dissatisfied and unhappy about the way we live and work. Pretty soon, we can't relax and enjoy life the way it is.

At the same time, we notice others enjoying life while allowing their flaws to show. We see them being OK with less than perfect results, and we either compare ourselves ("I'm better than he is") or criticize ourselves ("What's wrong with me? Why can't I be like that?").

It starts a vicious cycle. We don't want to be rejected, so we get defensive when other people criticize us. We try to protect our image of perfection. But that defensiveness drives people away from us. When that happens, we become critical of others, evaluating them against our own standards of perfection for ourselves. A sense of pride develops, and we hide our flaws even more, which makes us more unapproachable—and the cycle continues.

Author Anne Lamott wrote, "I think perfectionism is based on the obsessive belief that if you run carefully enough, hitting each stepping-stone just right, you won't have to die. The truth is that you will die anyway and that a lot of people who aren't even looking at their feet are going to do a whole lot better than you, and have a lot more fun while they're doing it."[2]

Perfectionism robs us of life's richness. If we're not willing to be human, we're more likely to become victims of the crazy people in our lives. We become less than ourselves because we're afraid someone will notice the flaws in our character and criticize us.

Confucius said, "Better a diamond with a flaw than a pebble without."[3]

Risking Recovery

If we've spent our whole life living for the approval of others, it's hard to break that pattern. That means we're living lives without authenticity. Strangely enough, we especially look for approval from the crazy people around us. They're the last people we would want controlling our lives, but we've given away the power of our own choices and emotions to them.

So, where do we go with all this? Here are some steps to consider:

1. *Recognize the damage that perfectionism does in our lives.* Take a piece of paper and divide it into two columns: "Advantages of Perfectionism" and "Disadvantages of Perfectionism." Put as many items in each column as possible. Your disadvantages column will probably be many times larger than your advantages column. If it's not, evaluate each of the advantages listed through the filter of truth. Are they really advantages, or are they just convenient and familiar?

2. *Challenge your thinking.* The Bible tells us to "take captive every thought" (2 Cor. 10:5). It's dangerous to assume that our perceptions are always accurate. Our emotions warp our view of reality. Each time we're tempted to try to appear perfect, we should ask ourselves, "Why am I doing this? What good will it do? What long-term damage is this process doing to my sanity and my relationships?"

3. *Ask yourself "What's the worst that could happen?"* So, our crazy person sees us as less than perfect, observing our mistakes or our humanness. "What's the worst thing that could happen?" we should ask ourselves. "And if it does happen, how bad would that actually be? How could we handle it?" We can admit our fears of being real.

4. *Accept the value of making mistakes.* In relationships, mistakes are how we learn and grow. People who won't give up striving for perfectionism are missing the building blocks of humanity that form a strong relationship. No one is perfect. That's why pencils have erasers.

5. *Go for 85 percent.* Perfectionists always strive for 100 percent and are disappointed when they can't achieve it or maintain it. But if they would change their standard to 85 percent, it's

usually possible to achieve or even exceed it. The result will still be excellent while allowing them to relax and enjoy the journey.

My longtime friend Matt called me one day with a problem. He's an executive with a major corporation, and at the time he was working on his master's degree at a university about fifty miles from his home. He's also the parent of four children and had commitments at his church.

"I don't know what to do," he said. "I get up and drive to work in traffic for about an hour, and then drive in traffic to school in the evening. Then I drive home late at night, and I'm falling asleep on the freeway because I'm so tired. I barely get to see my wife and kids, plus I have to study to keep up my A average in my classes and give 100 percent at work. I'm managing to do it all, but I'm exhausted. I don't know what to do, because they're all important."

"So, why are you going for straight A's?" I asked.

"Well, it's important to do everything with excellence. It wouldn't be right to do less than my best in anything."

I responded, "But it sounds like your family is the part of your life that's missing out the most. You're getting A's in school, but you're getting a B or a C in family. What if you reversed those and went for straight B's in school and an A in family?"

"I don't know if I could do that," he said.

"I've had my doctorate for twenty years," I continued. "In those twenty years, I've been asked many times where I studied and what field the degree was in, but no one has ever asked me what grades I got in any classes. I probably had a high B average, but I got the exact same degree as classmates who got straight A's. The goal was the degree and the gaining of knowledge. I was able to accomplish that goal without the pressure of striving for perfection."

Matt tried it, and it worked. By taking the pressure off himself to be perfect in school, he was able to devote more time to his family. His relationships at home improved as well as his performance at work.

He went for a B average at school—and actually ended up closer to an A average anyway.

He let it go.

Relaxing for Results

Whenever we try to appear perfect to crazy people, we're ensuring that our relationship will never be healthy. It's not based on truth; it's based on a contrived image we've developed. Without truth, the relationship will always be stalled. We're going for an A in image, but getting a C in connection.

What if we went for an A in being ourselves? What if we focused our energy on becoming genuine?

Actor Jim Carrey starred in a movie called *Liar, Liar* in which he lost the ability to tell a lie. No matter what he was asked, he had to tell the truth. When I saw that movie, I thought of how painful it would be if I couldn't conceal my true feelings when I wanted to.

But then I thought, *Why?* Being genuine doesn't mean just blurting out every negative thought we have about another person. What if we could be caring enough to "speak the truth in love" (see Eph. 4:15)? We wouldn't have to avoid conflict and confrontation out of fear; rather, we could be ourselves with integrity. It's really the only basis for healing a hurting relationship.

Maybe it's time to let go.

21

You Can't Steer a Parked Car

It's one week before the holiday, and your crazy person is going to be at the family gathering. You know how uncomfortable it has been in the past, trying to remain pleasant with them while you're dying on the inside. You'd like to avoid them but know that's not possible. You rehearse your encounter with them over and over during the next week, anticipating the worst while hoping for a miracle.

It's a miserable week.

After arriving at the event, you see them walk toward you. Your encounter with them is brief and cordial, but you're relieved when they walk away to talk with someone else. By the time the event is over, you're emotionally exhausted. The relationship isn't any better, but it isn't any worse. You survived, but your crazy person held your heart hostage for that entire week. You think, "OK, that's over. At least I don't have to go through that for a while."

But it took a lot of energy to get ready for that encounter. Even though it wasn't comfortable, the hardest part was done: the conversation had taken place. If you knew you had to see them again the next day, it would be a little easier because you survived the first conversation. You could simply build on that one without having to get geared up again.

It's called *inertia*. In physics, inertia means that an object tends to stay exactly where it is unless another object makes it move. Once it's in motion, it tends to stay in motion until something intervenes to stop it. It still requires a little work to keep it moving, but only a fraction of what it took to set it in motion. If that work doesn't take place, the object gradually slows down and ends up where it started.

In relationships, inertia means that nothing changes unless someone starts the process. Once that action is taken and there is some movement in the relationship, it takes a lot less action to keep it going. But if no action takes place, the relationship reverts back to where it started.

We understand that it takes a lot of energy to begin working on an unhealthy relationship. But do we *want* to keep it moving? That's a valid question, because we don't have any guarantees about where it will go once it's in motion.

When I was in high school, my first car was a 1967 Chevy Camaro. It wouldn't start one day as it sat in my parents' driveway, and a friend and I decided to hotwire the ignition. It was a fairly simple task, since older cars didn't have antitheft devices. We opened the hood and connected a wire from the starter to the battery, bypassing the ignition switch.

It worked. The car started. But it lurched forward, and we realized that we had forgotten to put the manual transmission in neutral. Since no one was in the car, it began a journey of its own. We scrambled to get inside and hit the brakes, but we didn't make it in time. The car finally stopped when it crashed through a fence near the end of the driveway.

That's like our fear in relationships. The hardest part is building up to those initial encounters. But once the connection begins, we're afraid it might take off and we'll lose control.

Why Bother Starting?

"OK, so I made the connection. But isn't that enough? If I avoid that person from now on, I can just skip the drama. Why bother?"

Building on that first encounter makes it easier to connect in the future. When we fail to build on those connections, the relationship always goes back to the way it was. Then, when we are forced into dealing with them again in the future, we have to start from square one because we haven't kept building.

We talked in earlier chapters about basing our emotional energy on the importance of the relationship. The closer someone is to us, the more emotional energy our relationship with them deserves. The less connected we are with a person, the less energy we should expend. We don't need to spend a lot of time with a stranger who criticizes our behavior, but we do need to invest in family, friends, or work associates whom we encounter each day.

People on the fringes of our lives should be dealt with in fringe ways; we should not allow them to be more than a blip on our radar screen. People who are more front and center because of their unavoidable connection require more attention. That doesn't mean we need to heal every unhealthy relationship simply because it's close. Rather, it means focusing enough energy to determine what the relationship should be like, coming up with a plan, and setting appropriate boundaries.

It's one thing to read books about becoming free from the impact that crazy people have on our lives. It's quite another to make it happen.

We've gotten used to quick fixes. When the car breaks down, we take it to a mechanic. It might be expensive, but we usually get our car back the same day and the problem is solved. Relationships don't respond to quick fixes. Working on relationships feels like trying to fix cancer; it's been growing for a long time unnoticed, it often requires drastic measures, and the outcome is uncertain.

When we see someone making totally crazy choices and exhibiting irrational behaviors, we tend to look at the surface impact. We forget that those patterns have been growing for a long time in their lives. That doesn't excuse their behavior, but it helps explain it.

A friend and I were discussing a co-worker who drove us crazy. We talked about the way she approached people, the manipulation and intimidation she used in most relationships, and how other people perceived her.

Then my friend said, "I wonder what happened."

"What happened to what?" I responded.

"What happened to her. I wonder what happened in her life that has brought her to the place where she feels like she has to act the way she does. It's not normal for people to act like that. Something happened."

That was a turning point for me. I still had to work with this person and had simply been seeing her as crazy. I wasn't thinking of the journey that took her to that point. I could keep avoiding her to keep my set point comfortable, but nothing would ever change. We would still have a shallow, unhealthy, superficial relationship.

Since I had to work with her, I decided to overcome inertia. Even though I still considered her to be crazy, I began to relate to her as a whole person. I didn't have to figure her out; I just needed to understand that there are reasons people become crazy and focus on how I would respond.

It took effort and risk for me to move in that direction. I determined what boundaries needed to be in place and planned my responses when she pushed those boundaries. I also had to look at my own contribution to the outcomes.

My co-worker still seems to be on a mission of making people crazy. However, by taking the time to carefully think through the relationship, I was able to develop a healthy way of relating to her. It took time and planning, and things still aren't comfortable. But the effort to keep that relationship healthy is just a fraction of the effort it would take to start over each time.

Finding Hope

When a relationship has been painful for a long time, we feel hopeless for any change to take place. We've learned to coexist with our crazy person; while that's not healthy, we no longer notice the pain because we've gotten used to it. We're afraid that if we start working on the relationship we'll stir something up that could be uncomfortable.

It's like being submerged in debt and going shopping to feel better. We're denying the reality of our financial situation by thinking, "Since I'm buying things, I must not be in financial trouble."

If we try to fix everything in our relationships overnight, we'll be overwhelmed with the magnitude of the task. But if we don't take any action, with either the crazy person's behavior or our own responses, there's no hope for healing on either side. It might take work to get a relationship moving, and there's no guarantee of where it will end up. But nothing will happen until we take the first step.

Overcoming inertia simply means taking the first step.

A Prescription for Progress

A strained relationship is already delicate, and we don't want to send it into a tailspin. When we choose to overcome inertia and work on our connection with that person, there are several steps in the process.

1. Develop an Honest Perspective

The reality in relationships is that they take time to grow. When things aren't right, we want to fix them. But there are no quick fixes between people. When we try to rush relationships, the healing slows down. When we allow time for healing, the process speeds up. That's why the first step in overcoming inertia is to live with the reality of each situation, not the fantasy of our desires.

2. Value Tiny Steps

Whenever we see a huge task ahead, we assume it will take more work than a small task. We don't even want to start because it seems overwhelming. A big task is simply a series of small tasks done in succession. We can't do every part of a project; we can only do one step. If we recognize that we can only do one step followed by another and another, we can accomplish huge things. Consistent small steps can have dramatic results and immediate payoff.

Relationships are the same way. The more painful and close a crazy relationship is, the more work it feels like it's going to be. It's futile to think of everything that could go wrong in the future. All we have is the current moment. Deal with one situation at a time. A single step isn't wasted effort; it's the beginning of a long journey in the right direction.

3. Believe in the Possibilities, but Accept the Way Things Are

Can our crazy person change? As long as they're alive, there is always hope. Something could happen, and that something could impact them in a way that could change their thinking and behavior.

That perspective has to be balanced with the fact that they might not change (and probably won't). If our happiness and sanity is based on the expectation of them changing, we've handed them the reins in our lives.

4. Don't Straddle the Centerline

It might seem safe to stay in the middle of the road, straddling the line between working on a relationship and leaving it alone. But staying in the middle is unhealthy because there is no progress in any direction. We're avoiding pain instead of pursuing health. We sidestep making a decision because we're afraid it will be the wrong one. However, it's better to make a decision and take action, then steer the results as they arise.

There's nothing in the middle of the road but yellow stripes and dead armadillos.

5. Live in the Present

While it's natural for us to focus on outcomes, that's a poor standard for evaluating relationships. Instead of judging results, we should celebrate progress. Our purpose is not to guarantee a healthy relationship; it's to determine what choices are best in the present, stay current, and focus on what's happening this moment. It's dangerous to wish for the past or fantasize about the future. When it comes to relationships, all we have is today.

6. Find the Big Picture

The crazier the relationship and the closer the person is to us, the more likely that they'll provide drama. But we are more than our relationships. We need to look through the lens of reality, seeing all of the things that make us human instead of judging ourselves by that one part of our lives.

Someone said we miss 100 percent of the opportunities we never take. If we let our relationships remain as they are, nothing will ever change. If we overcome inertia, we have hope for the journey.

We need to take the first step.

22

Your Relationship Survival Kit

Whenever I travel and people find out I live in Southern California, they often ask, "How can you live where there are earthquakes?" They're terrified at the thought of the ground shaking because they've never experienced it.

My response is, "I'd rather have earthquakes than some other natural disaster. With tornados and hurricanes, you know hours ahead of time they might be coming, so you're constantly dreading them and wondering when they might hit. With an earthquake, you have no idea that it's coming until it starts. By the time you figure out what it is, it's probably over. If you're still alive, you're OK. You might have some damage, but you start cleaning it up."

I think toxic relationships are like that. You might be going along fine for a long time, when out of the blue, the crazy person "strikes." They say something or do something that you weren't expecting, and you're left in a pile of emotional rubble. You survived, but you have to pick up the pieces.

Knowing that, how do we prepare for emotional earthquakes? We can't stop them from occurring, but we can get ready ahead of time so we know what to do when they strike.

When an earthquake hits California, you can go to any home improvement store an hour later and find fresh displays of "earthquake preparedness kits." They sell like hotcakes because people have just realized how unprepared they were. If the quake had been bigger, they wouldn't have been ready for the level of damage or the loss of utilities and basic services.

Earthquake preparedness kits contain the essentials to survive for several days if you're cut off from help: water, food, can opener, plates and utensils, first aid supplies, clothing, personal hygiene items, blankets, and so forth. People usually don't purchase these things until the quake happens and they're reminded of the need to get ready.

A Checklist of Supplies

In this book, we've talked about the futility of expecting another person to change. It's possible, but we can't count on it. The only guarantee we have in relationships is changing ourselves, becoming the type of people who can handle the chaos that others bring into our lives.

Knowing that people will bring drama into our lives unexpectedly, we need to get ready. As with earthquakes, we don't know when that dramatic situation will happen, but we're confident that it will. Rather than waiting until it occurs, true survival depends on getting our supplies in order.

What do we need in our relationship survival kit? Here are the basics:

We Need Perspective

Jerry is driven by performance. Some people would call him a workaholic, but he believes he's just carrying out a standard of excellence. He gets to the office early, brings work home at night, and constantly checks his smartphone on weekends to stay in touch. His family appreciates him being there at night and on weekends, but they wish he was there mentally and emotionally as well.

"It's just part of the job," he says. "I hate the time and pressure it takes, but it's the only way to stay on top."

Unfortunately, that lifestyle has gotten out of control. Jerry agreed to marriage counseling when he saw the damage that was happening to his closest relationships, and he genuinely wants help. But he doesn't see any way out of the work situation.

After several sessions, Jerry began to see the reason for his perspective. As a child, he wanted to please his domineering father. The only time he received praise from his dad was when he was productive and accomplishing something. Any time he took a break, his dad would call him lazy and tell him he was using up oxygen that a productive person could be using.

His father has been gone for twenty years, but Jerry is still trying to please his dad through his performance, having never experienced unconditional love.

When we look at ourselves honestly, most of us discover that there are hidden reasons why we do what we do. We relate to others through the lenses we've developed and wonder why nothing ever changes. The crazy people in our lives seem to be the problem, and we feel like our pain is because of their behavior.

It's time to correct those lenses. Our lenses provide our perspective. If our perspective is wrong, our relationships won't work.

We Need Other People

The problem with self-help books is that we're trying to solve our problems without having anyone else coming alongside. We have a problem that we don't know how to solve, but then we try to solve it alone (following the suggestions in the book).

Books are great, but they're no substitute for human interaction. When we're caught in the emotional chaos of our lives, we need someone else to challenge our perspective, provide insight, and ask the right questions.

Sometimes people connect with others for the sole purpose of complaining about their crazy person, hoping that they'll get some emotional support. That's no way to find a solution; it's simply gossip. However, the old adage "Two heads are better than one" is appropriate; bringing multiple minds to the situation keeps our thinking clear.

Deep-seated pain might need more than supportive, challenging friends. When the impact of crazy people in our lives becomes over-whelming, that's usually a sign that it's time for professional help. There's no shame in going to a psychologist or therapist to sort through tough issues any more than in going to a skilled mechanic to help us fix problems with our car. They're experts, and their training and experience have prepared them to diagnose and treat issues we don't recognize.

We Need Boundaries

When people use mind games to try manipulating us, knowing how to respond takes away the pressure when it happens. We'll still feel the emotion in the moment, but we'll recognize their tactics when they occur. Boundaries are like fences; when we've put them in place, it helps keep intruders from invading our sanity.

Boundaries are the decisions we've made that protect our emotions. When someone crosses a boundary, we don't have to get upset; we simply restate the boundary and stick to it. The other person might get upset and try to manipulate us, but we keep calmly reiterating the boundary we've established.

Jill loves her husband, John, but her mother constantly finds fault with him in her conversations with Jill. There might be a lot of truth in what she's saying, but Jill finds herself feeling more and more nega-tive toward John after those discussions. She realizes that her mother's input is poisoning her attitude toward her husband.

So she sets a boundary, deciding that she won't listen to any more negative input about John. The next time her mother starts to bring up her concerns, Jill says, "You know, Mom, I really love John and believe in him. When you talk about all the things that are wrong with him, I realize that it's not healthy for me, and it's messing with my attitude. It's not fair to John, because you really need to be talking to him about your concerns, not me. So I need you to have those conversations with John from now on instead of me."

If her mother says, "I can't talk to him about those things," Jill could use her boundary: "I'm really sorry you feel that way, but it really needs to be between you and him."

If her mother says, "That's ridiculous. I'm just trying to help," Jill could say, "I'm sorry, but I really can't have those conversations anymore."

If her mother uses guilt and says, "Well, if you don't want to talk to me, I just won't call anymore," Jill could respond, "I'm sorry you feel that way, and I would miss our conversations. There are lots of other things we can talk about, but I just won't be going there about John."

That's the value of planning ahead. We can respond without emotion if we know our boundaries. Even when the other person gets upset or tries to manipulate us, we simply state our boundaries over and over. We don't have to explain or justify them. We just have to stick to them. Boundaries become a tool we can use to form the structure of relationships that work.

We Need Examples

Many people grew up without healthy relationships. Their models demonstrated the wrong way to connect with others, and it's the only way they know how to relate. They're often the ones who feel the need to fix everyone around them, and they base their own self-worth on what others do or say. They haven't learned to let others take responsibility for their own choices.

However, my wife's parents demonstrated this masterfully. Looking back over the early years of our marriage, Diane and I made some pretty crazy choices. We thought they were good at the time, but we recognize in hindsight how foolish we were. We survived but made a lot of mistakes along the way.

They were *our* mistakes. Diane's parents probably had some long private conversations about the insane things we were doing, and I'm sure they wanted to jump in and tell us what we were doing wrong. Still, they didn't interfere. Sometimes they expressed their concerns in the form of questions ("Have you thought about this?"), but they always hung in there with us no matter what choices we made. They knew it was our life, and they let us make own our decisions.

The result? They laid the foundation for us to have a healthy, loving relationship with them. We think they do some pretty crazy things themselves, but it's their life and their choices, not ours.

If we haven't had good examples, it's worth the effort to seek them out. It might be a family member who connects well with others, a friend's relative whom they recommend, or a respected couple from church. We can make an initial contact for coffee or a casual backyard dinner. It doesn't have to involve a deep interrogation of their techniques. Simply getting to know them over time gives us the chance to learn from their informal mentoring.

We Need Encouragement

When speed bumps appear in relationships, it's natural to get discouraged. We have great intentions to keep a positive attitude, but it disappears during a relational crisis. Just when we thought things were improving and we were responding well, our emotions take a nosedive.

Discourage means "dis-courage"—to take the courage out of someone. We lose our courage to stay focused and positive, and we have trouble replacing it by ourselves. It's like walking through a dark forest or down a deserted street at night. It's scary on your own, but much less threatening when you've got someone next to you sharing the experience. That's when we need *encouragement*—someone to put the courage back in.

We can't do that alone. In times of discouragement, we need people we trust to build into our lives. They provide the courage when we can't provide it for ourselves.

Where can we find someone to fill our tank when it's empty?

- Think through the people who have encouraged you in the past. They're probably the ones who were better at listening than at giving advice. If you can't think of someone, ask a trusted friend who it is that encourages them and ask for an introduction.
- Send an email or call that person. Don't go into a lot of detail; just invite them out for coffee and let them know you need a listening ear.
- If they say their schedule is tight, don't assume they don't want to talk to you. Assume they're telling you the truth and don't have the time. Then, look for someone else.
- Don't ask or expect them to fix everything. Just be grateful for someone to walk beside you during a tough journey.

No one can predict an earthquake. No one can tell us when a painful encounter might happen. In both cases, the key is to be prepared. Preparation takes place *before* the earthquake takes place, not after.

The earthquake is coming. It's time to shop for supplies.

23

It's Worth the Effort

It's been said that you can watch a six-year-old and tell what they're going to be like when they're an adult. They'll grow and mature over time, but their basic temperament has been established. If they're on the quiet side at six, they'll probably be reflective and deep in their relationships in their sixties. If they're outgoing, they'll be the one coordinating the neighborhood barbecue later in life. If they love order and detail, their car will always be waxed and everything in their home will be exactly in place.

That doesn't always happen, but it's usually the outcome. If we observe the uniqueness of our kids, we can capitalize on those characterics as they grow. If we try to change them and force them to become something they're not, we're setting them (and us) up for frustration.

Aaron is concerned that his son seems introverted and wants to help him become more outgoing. So he tries to force him to respond to situations in more outgoing ways. He means well, but his son is uncomfortable in those situations and assumes something is wrong with him that needs to be fixed.

It's appropriate to teach social skills, provided we follow the contours of a child's basic wiring. An introvert will never become an extrovert and vice versa. Instead, they need to learn how to be the best introvert or extrovert they can be, utilizing their unique strengths and gifts.

My six-year-old granddaughter, Averie, spends the night at our house on a regular basis. Her routine is always the same: she walks in the door and heads straight back to her room where she unpacks her suitcase, lays out her clothes for the next day, arranges her toys in the order she wants to play with them, and makes sure everything is in order. That happens in the first two minutes. Getting everything organized frees her to come out and play, knowing that it's all taken care of.

Some people might think she's crazy, and her parents could try forcing her to lighten up for fear she'll end up with compulsive behaviors. But that's because they would be looking at her through their lenses and putting their expectations on her.

Don't we do that with other people? We all have crazy people in our lives, and we've talked about how efficient they are at ruining our lives. We assume that they need to change. But even though we're bugged by their behavior, freedom comes when we accept their basic wiring instead of trying to make them become like us.

The Source of Craziness

Ask any group of kindergarten kids, "How many of you are artists?" Every hand goes up. Pose the same question to eighth graders and you'll see about one-third of the hands. Ask a group of adults, you'll find one or two.

What happens between kindergarten and adulthood? Somebody changed the child's lenses. Maybe she drew a picture and a well-meaning adult said, "Here, let me show you how to draw it better."

So she thinks, "I guess I'm not an artist after all. Only adults can draw." Children don't have the inner resources to question adults, so they form their value based on the opinions of others. Years later, they still believe those opinions.

Most people remember the title *Grumpy Old Men*, even if they never saw the movie. It's a description we easily identify with because we've all known older people who seem to be bitter about where life has taken them. They're set in their ways and angry about the past. As much as they need the affection of other people, their grumpiness drives others away.

We've made choices throughout our lives that determine who we are in the present. Sometimes early choices were made for us, such as abandonment or abuse. Whether good or bad, those choices determine if we're viewing life through positive or negative lenses. If we think life is miserable, it probably has more to do with our lens than with reality.

With a negative lens, we're usually suspicious. When someone does or says something, we're always looking for their hidden intent. We assume they're trying to mess up our lives on purpose.

That's the bad news: those lenses determine how we see the world, which determines how we feel. Yes, there are people doing crazy things, and we feel like they're ruining our lives. But another person can watch that same behavior and not take it personally.

Here's the good news: *we don't have to live as victims. We can change our lenses and think differently. Our relationships can be different than they are. There is hope.*

A New Lens for Relationships

It doesn't matter how long our emotions have been managed by crazy people. We can choose to live differently. Maybe other people *have* messed up our lives. But if we continue to live at the mercy of others in the future, it's our own fault. We have the ability to make different choices.

Sound unrealistic? The more deep-seated those patterns are, the bigger the task feels. But change is still possible. The perspective we've carried for years might need the objective view of a therapist or counselor trained in sorting through the rubble. As long as we're willing to begin the journey, there is always hope.

Your local bookstore carries a lot of books with tips for surviving crazy relationships. But if we're looking through negative, self-defeating lenses and don't take ownership of our choices, the tips won't work. It's an inside out job; it has to start with us. If we want our relationships to change, *we* have to change.

That doesn't mean rolling over and playing dead, saying the other person is right and we're wrong. That's not realistic. It means we look inward first and become the type of person we need to be, making sure we're viewing things through the right lenses. From that foundation, we'll have the inner strength to handle the crazy people in our lives.

Think of the benefits that come from having a healthy perspective on life:

- *People will like us better.* No one is attracted to a grumpy, negative person.
- *We'll like ourselves better.* We'll wake up each morning with a sense of anticipation, knowing that we can handle the craziness that will inevitably happen during the day.
- *Our emotions will be more real.* People will still push our buttons, but we'll have the internal resources to handle it.
- *We'll have perspective.* It will be easier to sort through everything that happens, determining what deserves our emotional energy and what we should let go.
- *We won't live as victims of other people and external circumstances.* We'll take back the reins of our lives that we've given to others.

Twelve Tips for Healthy Relationships

Let's review some of the key concepts involved in setting groundwork for a new beginning:

1. *Learn to separate a person's crazy behavior from the rest of who they are.* Everyone does things that might be considered crazy, including us. But that's not all of who we are. We have good traits as well as bad, and we're in process. It's important to see others accurately if we're going to deal with them effectively.
2. *Recognize that change is always possible.* No one is hopeless, and change is always possible. It's true of us, and it's true of crazy people.
3. *Don't take responsibility for other people's choices.* We can try to influence them, but we can't do the hard work of change for them. It's their job, and we do them a disservice when we try to rescue them and take over.
4. *Don't put expectations on other people.* We can't depend on what someone else might do, because they might do something different. Expectations can lead to disappointment.
5. *Remember that there are no guarantees.* No matter how much energy and commitment we put into another person, we can't assume that there will be a happy ending. We can only make decisions about our own happiness and choices, regardless of what happens to the other person. Sure, we'll feel the pain of their poor choices, but it won't define us.
6. *Realize that you can't change the past, but you can change how you respond to it.* The past is permanent. No matter how painful the results of our past choices, they are behind us. Once we accept the reality of those choices instead of wallowing in them, we become free to move into the future.
7. *Believe that there is hope for the future.* Change is always possible. We can look through new lenses that can lead to an entirely new future. It might involve other people changing, but it might

not. We might be the only ones who change, but it will take us in new directions.

8. *You don't have to be a victim.* Even if we have spent years being controlled by the choices of others, we can learn new ways to think that lead to personal victory—no matter what other people do.

9. *Change takes time.* Like the story of the tortoise and the hare, persistence is more powerful than a quick, massive effort at reform. Healing relationships can't be rushed, and real results come from long-term commitment.

10. *There is no reward without risk.* Any time we try a different approach with our crazy relationships, we don't know how it will turn out. But taking those risks is the only way to break through the barriers that have been in place for so long. The best mountaintop views only come to those who take the risk of climbing.

11. *Preparation has great value.* The crazier the relationship, the more important it is to plan ahead for each connection. If we think carefully about each conversation before it happens, we won't be as easily manipulated.

12. *Choose to respond instead of react.* People do bad things, say words that hurt, and make accusations that devastate us. We're human, so we will have emotional reactions to those events. The key is to pause, notice our reactions, and then choose how we will respond. That brief moment allows us to steer our emotions, channeling them into the healthiest response.

Getting Professional Help

The principles we've talked about in this book aren't rocket science. They're just common sense and have been shaped through my interactions with people and their issues over the past thirty-five years. Simply stated, the principles work because they're based on truth, specifically God's truth presented in the Bible.

The Bible isn't a book about religion; it's about relationship. It's not a collection of dos and don'ts, but rather a practical guide for everyday living. There are a lot of books about relationships, but I haven't found anything that provides as much realistic, practical advice as the Bible. Since God designed relationships, it makes sense to read the owner's manual when something goes wrong.

That's why there is always hope in relationships. No matter how crazy someone is, God never gives up on them. He cares deeply about them as well as us, and he is working around the clock to influence change in their lives. When we can't take another step and feel hopeless, God promises to always be there. We probably qualify as crazy people in God's eyes, but he doesn't give up on us. Study how God relates to us and you'll learn how to relate to others.

Pick up a Bible and read the book of Proverbs. Type out every principle you can find that talks about relationships and try them out. You'll learn more about handling relationships from that than from any other source.

Choosing to Change

Jason and Jenny always heard that when you join a small group, someone in that group will be crazy. Those crazy people are the ones whose lives tend to be more high-maintenance, bringing drama to every group encounter. So Jason and Jenny were surprised when they formed a Bible study group with five other couples and no one was crazy. Then the realization hit: "Everybody in the group is normal—so that leaves us. We must be the crazy ones."

"They're everywhere!" you say. "I'm surrounded by crazy people!" It often feels like that, doesn't it? When we feel that way, we try to figure out how to avoid them or change them. That might work for a little while, but not long-term.

To get long-term results, the place to start is with ourselves. We can begin a journey of healing for our craziest relationships. The other person might stay crazy, but we'll have the resources to handle it without losing our minds.

It begins with the smallest step, not with trying to change everything. What would be one thing we could do this week that would start the process?

We have a choice. We can keep things the way they are, or we can start a journey to make things better. Maybe the other person changes; maybe we change. Maybe both of us change. There's always hope if we make new choices. We don't have to be victims.

People can't drive us crazy if we don't give them the keys.

Notes

Chapter 3 How Relationships Work

1.Kathy Collard Miller and D. Larry Miller, *When the Honeymoon's Over* (Wheaton: Shaw, 2000), 8.

Chapter 4 Stop Yelling at the Toaster Oven

1. Chip Heath and Dan Heath, *Switch: How to Change Things When Change Is Hard* (New York: Crown Business, 2010), 7–9.

Chapter 5 The Impact of Influence

1. As told in David Atkinson, *Leadership—By the Book* (Maitland, FL: Xulon Press, 2008), 65.

Chapter 7 Why Can't Everyone Be Like Me?

1. Marcus Buckingham and Curt Coffman, *First, Break All the Rules* (New York: Simon & Schuster, 1999).

2. James Stuart Bell and Jeanette Gardner Litteton, *Living the Serenity Prayer: True Stories of Acceptance, Courage, and Wisdom* (Avon, MA: Adams Media, 2007), 3.

Chapter 8 The Energy of Emotions

1. Shakespeare, *Hamlet*, act 2, scene ii.

Chapter 11 Key #2—Take Yourself Lightly

1. Tal Ben-Shahar, "Big Think Interview with Tal Ben-Shahar," September 23, 2009, http.//bigthink.com/ideas/16653.

2. Tony Snow, "Cancer's Unexpected Blessings," *Christianity Today Online*, July 20, 2007, www.christianitytoday.com/ct/2007/july/25.30.html.

Chapter 12 Key #3—Don't Sweat the Wrong Stuff

1. Richard Carlson, *Don't Sweat the Small Stuff . . . and It's All Small Stuff* (New York: Hyperion, 1997).

Chapter 14 Key #5—Live Through the Lens of Kindness

1. John Donne, *Devotions upon Emergent Occasions Meditation XVII* (Montreal: McGill-Queens University Press, 1975).

Chapter 15 Key #6—Base Your Choices on Integrity, Not Convenience

1. Quoted in Don Soderquist, *Live, Learn, Lead to Make a Difference* (Nashville: Thomas Nelson, 2006), 141.
2. Mark Twain, *Mark Twain's Notebook* (London: Hesperides Press, 2006), 240.

Chapter 16 Key #7—Go the Distance in Relationships

1. Haya El Nassar and Paul Overberg, "Fewer Couples Embrace Marriage; More Live Together," *USA Today*, May 26, 2011, http://www.usatoday.com/news/nation/census/2011-05-26-census-unmarried-couples_n.htm.
2. "Famous Quotes of Vince Lombardi," copyright 2010 by the Family of Vince Lombardi, www.vincelombardi.com/quotes.html.

Chapter 17 Prioritize Your Relationships

1. Quoted in Richard Koch, *The 80/20 Principle: The Secret of Achieving More with Less* (New York: Doubleday, 1998), 164.

Chapter 18 No Guarantees

1. Zig Ziglar, 1-Famous-Quotes.com, http://www.1-famous-quotes.com/quote/18406.
2. Erma Bombeck, BrainyQuote.com, http://www.brainyquote.com/quotes/quotes/e/ermabombec136528.html.

Chapter 20 Giving Up on Getting Straight A's

1. John Powell, *Why Am I Afraid To Tell You Who I Am?* (Chicago: Argus, 1969), 11.
2. Anne Lamott, *Bird by Bird: Some Instructions on Writing and Life* (New York: Anchor Books, 1995), 28.
3. Confucius, BrainyQuote.com, http://www.brainyquote.com/quotes/quotes/c/confucius107048.html.

Mike Bechtle has a unique blend of ministry and corporate experience—from eighteen years in churches and Christian universities to more than 2900 time- and life-management seminars taught to many of the Fortune 500 companies. He is the author of *Confident Conversation* and *Evangelism for the Rest of Us*, and his articles have appeared in publications such as *Discipleship Journal*, *Moody*, *Eternity*, Pastors. com, and *Entrepreneur*. He has been speaking at churches and conventions since 1974. After receiving his master's degree from Talbot School of Theology, he earned his doctorate in higher and adult education from Arizona State University. Currently a senior training consultant for FranklinCovey Company, he lives in Fullerton, California. For more information about speaking engagements and seminars, visit:

www.mikebechtle.com
www.thecrazypeoplebook.com